GOLDEN HARVEST in Ghana

GOLDEN HARVEST in Ghana

Gospel Beginnings in West Africa

Marjorie Wall Folsom

ISBN: 0-88290-347-0
Library of Congress Catalog Card Number: 89-083741
Horizon Publishers' Catalog and Order Number: 2002
First Printing: May, 1989

Printing: 1 2 3 4 5 6 7 8 9 10

Printed and distributed
in the United States of America by

Horizon Publishers
& Distributors, Incorporated
P.O. Box 490 Bountiful, Utah 84010-0490

Acknowledgments

My love and appreciation is extended to

— my dear husband and missionary companion, whose patience and "long-suffering" during the compilation of this work, along with his judgment and invaluable advice, made it a labor of love;

— to Thomas S. Gill, for his generous and honest review of the manuscript;

— to Edmund Kwame Tawiah, my Ghanaian "son," for his verification and enthusiastic encouragement;

— and to all who have shared their testimonies and contributed their love and generosity toward whatever has inspired these pages.

Contents

Preface

THE PARABLE OF THE PIANO KEYS

You can play a tune of sorts on the white keys
And you can play a tune of sorts on the black keys
But for harmony you must use both the black and the white.
(Dr. A.G. Aggrey, quoted in Ghana: Past and Present
by Americo Samassa Mayer.)

A persistent feeling within, almost a compulsion, has finally persuaded me to bring together some experiences and impressions which have become part of our lives.

Distilled within my soul is a sure knowledge of the divinity of the Savior, of the love which he and our Heavenly Father have for each of us even in "the uttermost parts of the earth"; that all are numbered and precious to him; that there is a plan irrevocably decreed for the benefit and salvation of all.

Therefore, out of love for the gospel, our Heavenly Father, our beloved family, and our far-off brothers and sisters, this offering may hopefully impart to its readers my testimony of the Lord's continual goodness and mercy.

To those distant-in-miles but close-in-spirit black brothers and sisters in West Africa, whose spiritual and sensitive souls have such great depth of beauty, I pay deepest tribute. In verity, their culture is of such richness that our so-called civilized world, about which we tend to be smug and self-righteous, thinking it the best and most advanced, would be greatly enhanced were we to emulate many of its attributes.

To be cultured is relative. If measured by the goodness of the heart, these gentle people would stand tall indeed. The tapestry of mankind, woven of the rich threads of each culture, is designed to grace and endow all. Indeed we will ever be blessed and enriched through the intertwining of their lives and love with ours.

1

Whiteman! Whiteman!

For behold the field is black already to harvest.
(Doctrine & Covenants 4:4, Paraphrased)

"Whiteman! Whiteman!"

Hearing these shouts, we spun around to see seven smiling clean-cut young men bounding down the sharp bluff with giant leaps. Eagerly they strode across the beach toward us, kicking up little spurts of sand with each step.

Their first words, "What are you doing here?" were typically straightforward. With natural candor, the Ghanaians delighted us with this oft-repeated but simple query which meant no offense. It afforded us the desired opportunity to reply in an equally direct manner, "We have come half-way around the world to bring you the restored gospel of Jesus Christ." Nods and smiles on their handsome black faces evidenced approval.

With all our hearts we had learned to love and appreciate these gentle and gracious people, so their instant reply came as no surprise, "Oh fine, that is what we want to hear. Please tell us about it." This too was typical, as young and old, in all stations of life, manifested interest in the Church. Without exception, all we encountered seemed sincere, displaying no restraint or guile in their quest for spiritual enlightenment. "Yes, of course," was our delighted rejoinder, "we will be happy to share the message of the restored gospel of Jesus Christ with you."

Truly prepared of the Lord, the people of Ghana were ready to receive his gospel, restored in its fullness for the last time and which is to all people, "unto the uttermost part of the earth." (Acts 1:8)

Here to the pristine shores of West Africa, at Komenda, Ghana, nearly 200 members of the Cape Coast branches of The Church of Jesus Christ of Latter-day Saints had gathered on 26 December, 1983, a Monday, for a Christmas picnic. Fellowshipping, eating, dancing to the beat of drums, playing soccer, and frolicking in the warm surf of the Gulf of Guinea, were part of a joyous day.

Having parked our van atop the bluff adjacent to the Komenda Teachers College which overlooked the beach, these men, seeing the Church's name with "Missionary" on the door panels, had come seeking missionaries. They were student teachers attending the college for a three weeks' seminar during their Christmas break from the schools where they taught.

Choosing a secluded area we soon formed a circle where, nestled crosslegged in the warm sand, the shaggy palm trees offered sanctuary from the equatorial rays. In addition to these seven teachers, we had invited Thomas Appiah Sr.; J.W.B. Johnson, original founder of the Church in Ghana and now supervisor over local district missionaries; and Kojo Amankwah, a newly-trained and dedicated district missionary, to join the group.

Although the teachers spoke English, they preferred their native language, Fante, as involved messages and information were more readily assimilated in their own tongue. After introductions and brief explanations, we were soon teaching the gospel, according to their expressed desire.

Elder Amankwah, speaking in Fante, presented the discussion, "Acceptance of Christ." As a part-time university student, he related well to them. With eyes riveted on him, they sat absorbed as new and profound light on the divine mission of the Savior unfolded. Acceptance of these concepts was revealed by expressive faces and approving nods, which vividly portrayed their inner feelings. Before long three others from the college joined the group. At the completion of this lesson and eager for more, the discussion on "Eternal Progression" was presented and equally well received.

The students' thoughtful questions and observations revealed their yearning to unravel life's meaning. One commented, "Other churches don't dig much into the Bible because they don't have the answers." Another said,"The ministers don't want you to read the Bible as they want to do all the thinking for you." And still another, "I jumped out of my church several years ago, dissatisfied with their teachings and lack of it in not wanting us to read the Bible; to depend only on what the priest chose to tell us."

Familiar with biblical contents as to chapter and verse, they marveled as their understanding expanded on passages that previously neither they nor their ministers had comprehended.

Facing a dilemma, the students desired to receive all seven lessons before school disbanded on Friday, but final exams were to fill the coming week. Nevertheless, a Wednesday appointment was set. For this lesson we were accorded the use of a college classroom. Their enthusiasm spread to their classmates, which nearly doubled the attendance on this occasion. Never have we experienced more fertile soil from which to garner a golden harvest.

As before, Elder Amankwah held a rapt and attentive class. Their faces reflected delight in hearing how the gospel was restored by the prophet Joseph Smith. Although their language was basically unknown to us, we felt no barrier to the Holy Spirit as unmistakably it had touched them. Many had been converted, having received but the first three lessons; some only one or two.

Reluctant for us to leave, they gathered around at the conclusion, plying us with questions. One suggested, "Now we can all go back to our villages and start up a church." He immediately yearned to do as the Savior admonished, "When thou art converted, strengthen thy brethren." (Luke 22:32) Again, this was typical of many we baptized. They desired to become missionaries, to share the testimonies and blessings that had so newly changed their own lives.

It became essential, therefore, before all departed their separate ways, that we convey to them an understanding of the doctrine and principle that all leaders are to be called of God; that they must have the proper authority bestowed upon them "by the laying on of hands by those who are in authority to preach the gospel and administer in the ordinances thereof." (Article of Faith 5) We emphasized that no one has authority to take it upon himself to represent the Lord even as he counseled his apostles, "Ye have not chosen me, but I have chosen you and ordained you." (John 15:16) and "No man taketh this honour unto himself, but he that is called of God, as was Aaron." (Hebrews 5:4)

When they dispersed, they seemed satisfied and happy to have learned the true order of conducting affairs in the Lord's kingdom. They too had the insatiable desire expressed by so many, "Teach me, teach me! Tell me what the Lord wants me to do." We found it gratifying that throughout our mission all desired and humbly accepted instruction as they struggled to learn their duties in whatever capacity or position they held. Truly they were "humble,...and submissive and gentle; easy to be entreated; full of patience and long suffering." (Alma 7:23)

Our minds continually paraphrased the scripture, "For behold the field is white already to harvest," to become the meaningful phrase in this land, "For behold the field is black already to harvest." (D & C 4:4)

Due to exams, this was the last lesson for these teachers at this time. On Friday they returned to their scattered villages, some in bush country (jungle as we might say), and others to urban areas, armed with some of these pearls of great price. We felt that the seeds planted in their hearts would flourish and expand in ever-widening influence. Later, a few of these teachers found their way back to us; were taught further and baptized.

How blessed and privileged we were to be in Ghana continuing the Lord's work. Even as shining rays of sunlight pierce the shrouds of darkness, the first two authorized missionary couples came in December 1978 and brought the power and authority of the restored gospel of Jesus Christ to a waiting and prepared multitude. With the arrival of these missionaries, Elders Rendell N. Mabey and Edwin "Ted" Cannon with their wives, Rachel and Janeth, our black brothers' and sisters' long vigil for truth and recognition had been acknowledged by the Lord. Their coming followed closely the event that made it possible.

On the 8th of June, 1978, President Spencer W. Kimball, beloved prophet of The Church of Jesus Christ of Latter-day Saints, announced a revelation on their behalf. After much prayer and petitioning, the Lord revealed to President Kimball "that the long-promised day has come when every faithful, worthy man in the Church may receive the holy priesthood, with power to exercise its divine authority, and enjoy with his loved ones every blessing that flows therefrom, including the blessings of the temple. Accordingly, all worthy male members of the Church may be ordained to the priesthood without regard for race or color." (D & C Official Declaration 2)

Their time had come. Silver linings hidden by those long-hovering clouds had broken through to dispel the shadows from a formerly dark continent.

The coming chapters will unfold how the Lord, through dreams, visions, and even miracles, has and is leading our brothers and sisters by the hundreds, yes thousands, in this land to find his gospel. Related also are fascinating customs, life styles, flora and fauna which we encountered, personal conversion testimonies, and our uniquely rewarding experiences among a gentle people.

In a land where hunger, drought and privation of almost all comforts are the norm for most, we found a great hunger and thirst for spiritual nourishment. The desire burns within them to find and drink of that living water promised by the Savior, that they may hunger and thirst no more. Into their lives this fountain of living water has imparted such commitment and dedication that parallels are hard to find.

We felt highly favored to be sent to this special vineyard, not only to share the gospel of Jesus Christ but also to erect a chapel unto the Lord—the first Latter-day Saint chapel to be built by the Church on Ghana's soil. This, also in answer to the Ghanaian saints' fervent prayers, would fulfill a dire need and become the first of many chapels in the land.

Indeed, the Lord has sown golden seeds into the hearts of some of the "lost tribes of Israel" and truly, "the field is *black* already to harvest".

2

Through the Years

"Other couples go on missions, you are going on an experience."

These words, spoken by Wayne Millet of the missionary department as we visited with him in his Salt Lake City office, were indeed prophetic. Just before we entered the Missionary Training Center (MTC) in Provo, Utah, Brother Millet confirmed that our assignment would be in Ghana, West Africa. Although we accepted calls to serve for 18 months in the Africa West Mission, our particular destination was unknown to us until that moment. The mission comprised two countries, Ghana and Nigeria, each equally mysterious and exciting to contemplate. A country with a population of thirteen million, and approximately the size of the state of Oregon, Ghana was previously known as Gold Coast. At independence from British rule in 1957 it adopted the legendary name Ghana.

Never in our wildest dreams could we have envisioned the adventures and blessings that lay ahead as we sat preparing for them in the MTC during those lovely June days in 1983. Although we previously had served two full-time missions for the Church, being in this facility was for us a new and wonderful experience in itself. Before going to the New Zealand Wellington Mission in December 1977 we received training in the old Missionary Home in Salt Lake City; and when called to the Missouri Independence Mission in 1980 our attendance in the MTC was not required.

To this facility, a self-contained small city where every need is met (housing, food, laundry, clinic and bookstore), hundreds of young men and women, and increasing numbers of older couples, come each week.

After special training, they depart prepared in both body and spirit to share the blessings of the gospel in many parts of the world and in dozens of languages.

Those assigned to English-speaking countries, as were we, remain about two weeks, whereas those who must learn a foreign language are there for about two months of intensive study. They are then usually able to teach the gospel quite fluently in their new tongue, truly one of the miracles of the gospel of Jesus Christ.

Our call to Africa was basically the same as for most missions—that of teaching the gospel, leadership training, and member work. However, soon after entering the MTC the member of the First Quorum of the Seventy who presided over Great Britain and Africa, Elder Derek A. Cuthbert, excited us with an additional assignment. We were to build the first Latter-day Saint chapel in Ghana!

The first chapel in Ghana! What a privilege to be going to this relatively undeveloped all-black country to build their first chapel. Our assignment was to Cape Coast where the first baptisms in Ghana had been performed on the ocean shore a brief four-and-a-half years previously.

Why us? How could we be so blessed? Our minds raced back through the years to review some of the qualifications that may have propelled us to this point.

Max must have inherited some of the architect-builder characteristics of his great grandfather, William Harrison Folsom, who served as Church architect for several years during the early days of the Church. Some of his beautiful buildings still stand and are preserved by the Utah State Historical Society.

Most of Max's life has revolved around building and designing in one field or another. Self-taught, he grew up during the depression with little means to attend college. His first major accomplishment in this area was building our own modest home after we married. It began from a one-car garage on the ranch in Leavenworth, Washington where he and his father were co-owners of a dairy. Always challenged, he kept home and ranch buildings upgraded.

After World War II, with the dairy business sold but still living on the ranch, Max worked for several years, first as bookkeeper and then as designer-draftsman, for a firm building orchard trailers, steel structures and machinery. But a change in ownership of this business necessitated finding employment elsewhere.

At this time, the Columbia Basin Irrigation Project in central Washington state was burgeoning, destined to lace a million acres of land with a network of canals to be fed from the rising waters behind Grand Coulee Dam. This frontier beckoned as a land of opportunity for a growing family. Max obtained employment on this project in the Ephrata, Washington area. So, packing worldly possessions and our four children, we ventured into this new field of construction.

Although knowing this type of work was transitory, we nevertheless had faith that a more permanent position would come along. Indeed it did, one cold, blizzardy, minus 30-degree day in January 1950. Severe cold and mountainous drifts of snow had closed down all construction on the project and prospects for work were most bleak. Through the snowdrifts to our home, in answer to prayer, trudged Robert R. Ries, Chief Engineer for Grant County Public Utility District (PUD). The position he offered Max was the beginning of a thirty year love affair with a new designing career in the field of electrical production, transmission and distribution.

The PUD, in its embryo stage of development due to the immense irrigation project, afforded ample opportunity for learning and advancement. Many of Max's innovative designs found ready acceptance in this expanding field.

From its inception he was involved in planning, designing and engineering for the largest project ever built up to that time by a PUD—the Priest Rapids and Wanapum Dams which spanned the mighty Columbia River to produce electric power to meet ever increasing demands.

During these years Max, as chairman of the Building Committee, was active in the construction of our Ephrata Ward chapel, which at that time was accomplished almost entirely with volunteer labor. At the chapel dedication Max was serving as bishop. Although working full time for the PUD, he also designed many homes and commercial buildings. For our own investment he designed and built a duplex for rental purposes, also a large workshop containing a drafting office.

When he retired from the PUD in 1976 as Transmission-Substation Design Engineer, we had already enjoyed a full rich life. But some of the best years were yet to come!

Now free to work full time in his own drafting and designing business, he worked mainly with residential contractors. Also, just one year before retiring he had been called as Stake Patriarch.

Raising a family of three sons, Philip, Greg and Brad; and four daughters, Sandra West, Diane Packham, Marianne Anderson, and Lisa Becker; along with church activity, kept us busily fulfilled. Max's major church positions, bishop's counselor, bishop, ward clerk, high councilor and patriarch, along with mine as Relief Society president (several times), Primary president, counselor in the auxiliaries, Sunday School music director and Stake Primary president, brought varied training.

As our children's college and mission years arrived also came the need for added income. A part-time job with the U.S. Department of Commerce, first as census interviewer and then as supervisor, contributed a new dimension to my life. Interviewing, counseling, and training both men and women in various cities of the western states added insight and understanding for all peoples. Civic committees, PTA activities, and other volunteer efforts also wove invaluable threads into the fabric of my life.

Many times during my travels and activities I felt the protecting hand of the Lord to bring me safely through. In one instance, flying to Portland, Oregon on assignment, the plane was twice struck by lightning in a fierce thunderstorm. It seemed that it would surely go down in an explosion as streaks of fire shot around it. It didn't, but this and other life-threatening incidents caused me to ponder whether perhaps the Lord still had work for me to do. As I recall my various experiences it may be what President Kimball had in mind when he said, "It is a testimony to me, whenever we are ready, the Lord will use us for his purposes."

How the Lord guides our destinies may be illustrated by the following account. One Sunday evening several years ago, Leslie Boyce, President of the Quincy Washington Stake, entered our chapel toward the conclusion of sacrament meeting and sat on the back bench. After the meeting, as I shook his hand, I felt a strange sensation. It was as though we were being transported above or away from the crowd, that he had something to tell me; but nothing was said other than a brief greeting. The elapsed time, which seemed to be two or three minutes, was in reality but a split second. I reflected upon this incident.

Later, when President Boyce called us to his office, he said to me, "Do you remember when I shook your hand after your sacrament meeting two weeks ago?" Assuring him the memory was vivid, he added: "As I took your hand that night the Spirit whispered, 'There is your new stake Primary president.' I had come to your ward to ask someone else to be the stake Primary president." My spirit must have been interviewed that night two weeks previously, as when the call came I felt prepared and was happy to accept it.

After nearly five enjoyable years in that position, the Lord again showed me I was needed in other fields. For the second successive year our stake Primary presidency was chosen to host leaders at a regional gathering of several stakes, where we were to instruct and present new materials for the coming year. The preliminary planning meeting for this event so impressed me that I knew we must expend every effort to accomplish the Lord's work. Driving home that day, the car literally seemed to float.

Throughout the next week, buoyed with an exquisite exhilaration, I felt as saints must have in times past, who shouted "halleluia" or such, when touched by the Spirit. I could barely restrain myself from doing so in like manner. Many perhaps became annoyed with my exuberance as I repeatedly proclaimed how we must be more diligent in doing the Lord's work, all the while feeling as if I would surely burst.

Early Saturday morning, one week after this meeting, with that feeling still bubbling within me, I was prompted to pick up an "Ensign," the Church's magazine. Again it seemed that my hand was directed as I flipped to the back pages. Almost immediately my eyes were drawn to a talk given at a Regional Representatives Seminar. Words seemed to leap from the page, that couples should prepare themselves to go on missions. As I read this, a voice, as unmistakably clear and distinct as any I have every heard, declared, "You must go on a mission."

As both of us held stake positions, Max as patriarch and I as stake Primary president, we consulted the next day with Robert A. Hammond, our stake president. We found the Lord's will still operating on our behalf. When told of our "call" President Hammond answered, "Aha, now I understand, Sister Folsom, why I couldn't call you in this week for an interview. You have been approved by the High Council to be the new stake Relief Society president. I tried many times to call you, but each time my efforts were thwarted." This was further evidence that the Lord knew where he wanted us at this time of our lives.

Our first mission, then, took us to New Zealand where we enjoyed many sweet experiences. Living and working among the Maoris, we discovered to our delight that love recognizes no color barrier. This came about so simply, bringing to us an awareness of our true feelings.

Our assignment of activation in addition to teaching prospective members brought several visits to the home of a Maori sister whose non-member husband neither we nor the young missionaries working in the area had met. On a subsequent visit to this home, however, we were pleased to meet her husband, who stopped in briefly.

In New Zealand, Maoris and "pakehas" (Maori name for whites) freely intermarry. So when the young missionaries were informed of our meeting the husband, they asked, "Is he Maori or pakeha?" Ah! We could not honestly remember, but decided he was pakeha. Yes, he was pakeha.

What a surprise a few days later when we again met this brother and found him to be a very dark, almost black, Maori. Happily, our minds had not catalogued or made distinction as to color or race.

We learned too that missionaries are assigned where the Lord wants them to be. As a child I recall my mother corresponding with relatives in New Zealand and obtaining some genealogy. When these older relatives died, with no one else interested in continuing writing, contact was lost.

Now, two generations later, I arrived in New Zealand armed with genealogical data on my two great-uncles and a directive from my mother (then 86 years old) to find their descendants. (I really thought this quite unlikely.) What great joy and amazement when we discovered, after some search and a small ad placed in the local paper, that many of these descendants were living in our area. It was in the town of Pahiatua (I had to practice that name before it would roll off my tongue), our first assignment, that these two uncles had settled after emigrating from Denmark. Here many of their children had been born and raised. Coincidence? Not in the Lord's work.

In New Zealand we learned to follow the prompting of the Spirit. After being transferred to a new area some forty miles distant, I arose one morning with the distinct impression that a man we had been teaching in our previous area needed our help. Driving there immediately, we found him so ill he could scarcely raise a hand or lift his head off the pillow. As we greeted him, he weakly said, "I knew you would come. I knew you would come. I have been praying that you would come and pray me a blessing." Shortly after Max gave this fine man a blessing, he walked to the door to bid us farewell.

We learned that in times of discouragement the Lord's encircling arms, though unseen, can be felt. This came also in New Zealand in this new area, where despite hard work, fasting, and praying by both the young missionaries and us, progress seemed to be at a standstill in both activation and teaching.

One night, in a dream, I was among a crowd but standing apart from any near contact. While waiting for events, which seemed slow in happening, I felt a touch on my shoulder to which I paid no attention. Then an arm slid along my shoulder to rest there. Quickly looking around, I saw no one, but immediately felt an assurance of the Lord's love and presence in times of need flood over me. That also seemed a turning point for progress and greater success in that area.

During the last month of our mission in New Zealand Max worked feverishly remodelling the old house used as a chapel in the small town of Foxton. The transformation into a more functional chapel was the delight of all.

During this time we came to realize there were yet some who lacked acquaintance with the Church. A charge account in the Church's name was set up at a local hardware store so that on completion one payment could be made. While making a purchase one day, a new clerk wrote out the bill and at his enquiry as to whom it should be charged, Max replied, "LDS Church." As the clerk graciously completed the transaction with "Thank you, Mr. Church," it brought chuckles and explanations.

At Adam-ondi-Ahman in Missouri, the scene of our second mission, Max's building and remodeling capabilities were again put to the test. Being the first missionary couple called from home to go to Adam-ondi-Ahman, we felt like true pioneers.

To be on the land where father Adam, the Ancient of Days, raised his family, and where, three years prior to his death he had called his righteous posterity together to bless them, was a humbling experience. (See D & C 107:53-56)

Several other couples subsequently arrived to help clean and beautify the Lord's land. Old buildings were razed, some remodeled, and new ones built. Irrigation and domestic water systems were installed and tens of thousands of trees and shrubs were planted in a nursery. This was in preparation for the grand council where Adam and all his righteous posterity who have held keys of the kingdom will report their stewardship just prior to the Savior's coming in glory. (See D & C 116)

It was here that Max felt the healing hand of the Lord. In the process of pruning to beautify some large oak trees which overhung a deep ravine by our home, he fell from one. Landing on his feet some eighteen feet below on the boulder-strewn slope, the sudden impact crushed a vertebrae.

In St. Joseph hospital, without a cast, he had to lie quietly while his back mended. As I stood beside his hospital bed several days after the accident, Max lay on his back with his eyes closed. Opening them, he asked if I had put my hand under his back and rubbed it. No, I hadn't. To which he replied, "But I felt someone slide their hand under my back and rub it." From that time to this no twinge, pain, or other discomfort in his back, from this cause or any other, has been felt.

With both of us coming from pioneer stock and being fourth-generation Church members, we appreciate with utmost gratitude the extraordinary sacrifices freely proffered by our progenitors. Sometimes life itself was required of them while defending and establishing the Lord's true Church in these latter days. We find the days of pioneering are not over.

Max and I have felt a yearning, even an urgency, to do our small part to bring the blessings we enjoy into the lives of others, wherever it takes us. We love the Lord and his gospel. We love our fine supportive family of seven children and (when called to Africa) 26 grandchildren. Two more were born while we served in Africa and three have been added since.

How we missed them, going a second time almost half a world away to again be pioneers, to build the first chapel in Ghana. Never would we have considered leaving them except for the firm knowledge that the gospel of Jesus Christ is true, having been restored for the benefit of all mankind. It is our duty and joy to help others find its blessings.

Being called to Africa stirred our imaginations, as even from earliest childhood mysterious tales of a relatively unknown and uncharted "dark" continent were spoken of in awed tones. And we chuckled, as cartoons of missionaries being boiled in big black pots, with spear-wielding natives dancing around, coursed through our memory.

As we prepared to leave, almost to Timbuctu, which as children was the epitome of the most remote place on earth, our hearts filled with excitement and love for our as yet unknown brothers and sisters.

3

Arrival in Africa

"His messengers shall go forth as upon wings of lightning, and thus thou shalt carry the gospel to foreign lands...to the lost tribes of Israel."
(excerpt from Max's patriarchal blessing, 1928.)

Arriving early for our 11 p.m. flight from the teeming Gatwick airport in London, there was no mistaking from which gateway we would depart. The convergence of colorfully arrayed black Africans afforded our first real glimpse of the culture of which we would soon be a part.

The beauty and richness of their flowing robes and suits captivated us. Many of the garments gleamed with interwoven gold or silver threads. Gold rings and jewelry that plentifully adorned fingers and chests bespoke wealth and perhaps high standing. Others dressed more plainly; some in western styles.

Studying their handsome faces and mannerisms nourished our previous feelings of love and excitement. Most were surrounded by large bulging bags and boxes which far exceeded the limit usually allowed passengers to carry on. Later we understood the desperate need for the small luxuries, even necessities, in those bundles that in some countries are almost non-existent. Had I been more aware of the plight I myself would have stuffed a few more bags.

As we watched this ever-changing scene with interest, our minds reviewed the events of the past weeks since leaving the MTC. At the request of Elder Cuthbert we had stopped over at the Church's area headquarters for Britain and Africa, in Solihull, near Birmingham, to receive special instructions in assembling an English-made prefabricated chapel. Although many valuable suggestions and directions were received in England, plans were changed and the pre-fab building idea abandoned in favor of one to be built on the site.

Finally, as the huge British Caledonian plane roared in takeoff and gained altitude, a congenial mood prevailed. The passengers, although packed in like proverbial sardines, settled down and relaxed as the plane droned on its way.

After what seemed a very short night, preparations were made in the pre-dawn hours to land at Lagos, Nigeria. Loaded with bags of sundry shapes and sizes, most passengers disembarked here. Only a scattering of us remained to continue the 45-minute flight to Accra, the capitol and largest city of Ghana.

At the equator the swift rise or dip of the sun might be compared to the opening and closing of a curtain. Visible now, the coastline sped below us. In places, dense forests stretched inland, while over the golden beaches palm trees bowed as in obeisance to the foaming waves that spread at their feet.

Nearing Accra, the panorama shifted to open savanna dotted with palm trees. Postage-stamp-size cultivated plots were scattered at random with huts nearby. Looking at this rather wild and little-used land, the thought of potential cultivation brought out the farm heritage in me.

As the plane came to rest we were thankful to finally arrive in the land we were prepared to call home for the next eighteen months. However our tenure was later reduced, as the missionary department considered one year to be ample under the existing rigorous conditions.

Among a sea of black faces and waving hands on the observation deck overlooking the tarmac, a few white ones stood out in vivid contrast. These latter, we presumed correctly, were here to meet us.

Leaving the comfort of the air conditioned plane, rivulets of perspiration soon coursed down my face and back. Not wishing to lose personal contact with our luggage, we struggled through the corridor as grasping hands on every side were eager to "help."

After clearing customs, immigration and immunization requirements, we were thrilled to meet our mission president, Sylvester Cooper Jr. and his wife Elizabeth, from Rexburg, Idaho. Accompanying them were the only two missionary couples in Ghana, Elders and Sisters Clark and Donna Nelson of Salem, Utah, stationed in the mission home in Accra, and Armand and Jean Williams of Clifton, Arizona, whom we had come to replace in Cape Coast.

The several miles of travel from airport to mission home afforded our first glimpse of life in Ghana. Homes from the almost palatial to the poorest makeshift huts were colorful and unique in this land of contrasts, as my journal recorded:

> One is immediately struck by the differences in lifestyles here. Crumbling clay hovels seem to provide shelter for many where open sewers, green with slime, meander past homes or shop doors. Large opulent homes protected by high walls nestle under the cooling shade of palms.
>
> Small shops constructed of scraps of tin, bamboo and boards front some streets where small tables on uncertain legs display pitifully scant wares. Moving along we see modern office buildings and shops.
>
> People walking everywhere. Both women and children with heavy loads of almost everything imaginable needed no steadying hand to balance them gracefully on their heads. Women with babies wrapped on their backs, in addition to loads on heads, struggle with pails of water in each hand. One senses the strain under which these thin and sinewy bodies fairly vibrate, while tendons like taut wires stand out as they pace their rhythmic steps.
>
> Gaily painted slogan-adorned rickety buses loaded to overflowing inside and on top seem to carry mostly women and their wares to market. Black fumes billow from exhausts as they lurch and sway in unsuccessful attempts to avoid the ever-present potholes.
>
> Over open fires in many yards, big pots of steaming food, stirred with long paddles, keep hungry looking children hovering nearby, bowls in hand.
>
> It is apparent many are poor; some draped in rags, their thin bodies testifying of malnutrition. Children wave and smile as we drive by, denoting a happy people. We had learned long ago in other countries and cultures that so-called material blessings do not of themselves bring happiness. In fact they are often a detriment.
>
> Already we feel at home among this industrious and happy people, who, it is obvious, make do with little of this world's goods.

The mission home, surrounded by a six-foot-high decorative concrete block fence with locking iron gate, was spacious, comfortable, and comparatively cool under coconut palms and papaya trees.

A humble, spiritual leader, President Cooper was endowed with patience and wisdom, necessary attributes in this part of the world where difficult circumstances are met head on. As much as possible, he spent equal time in Nigeria and Ghana, the two countries comprising this mission.

These two countries were separated by two other small narrow countries, Togo and Benin, but the border between Ghana and Togo was closed to all traffic or trade. This necessitated air travel, which, never free from problems and vexations, made their almost-monthly trips major contests of endurance.

Our orientation to this unique mission contained many wise precautions and guidelines. Some medical advice essential to our health was:

1. Take malaria pills regularly every week, on the same day.
2. Beware of fresh-water parasites present in some streams.
3. Don't hang clothes outside to dry, as flies deposit eggs on the clothes. Then, as they hatch, the larvae will penetrate the skin.
4. Do not take sit-down baths.
5. Keep updated on gamma-globulin shots every 3 months.
6. Keep updated on cholera shots every 6 months.
7. Boil all drinking water for 20 minutes, then filter it.
8. Soak all vegies and some fruits for 30 minutes in milton (chlorine) solution.
9. Use milton water for both washing and rinsing dishes.
10. Precautions when eating locally prepared foods are warranted.

Personal safety precautions also were given:

1. Travel together at least two in a car at all times. Don't be diverted.
2. Keep the car in good repair for safety.
3. When taking pictures or tapes, obtain permission first.
4. Keep outside lights on all night.
5. Register with the American Embassy.
6. Obtain an alien card.

Many other common-sense precautions were advised to aid us as strangers in a new culture.

Although we were eager to begin our assignment, this was not yet possible. Patience, we found, is an attribute we were to cultivate assiduously. Some of our bags, shipped air cargo from London, had not arrived. The weight allowance in effect as we departed America was no longer valid when we left England two weeks later. If all our luggage had been taken with us as we left England it would have cost an extra $1200. Instead, $310 was paid to have three bags shipped air cargo on the next convenient flight. After five anxious days the bags arrived intact. And having entered the country without permanent visas, with only two-week visitors' permits, we were confronted with the prospect of having to leave every two weeks until permanent ones could be obtained.

If the first Sunday in Accra was a prelude to coming events, we knew that spiritual feasts were in store for us:

> Two of the finest sermons I have ever heard on the subjects of "Sacrament" and "Talents" were delivered by converts of only two weeks. Their ease of delivery, depth of message, and testimony were an indication of the level of their conversion. These beautiful people are without guile. They are taught by the Spirit and speak by the Spirit. What a thrilling mission this will be. (*Journal.*)

Before leaving for Cape Coast another hurdle remained: petrol (gasoline) for the car. Finding petrol, we discovered, was a constant and avid pursuit. On the eighth day after arrival, with petrol finally obtained, we excitedly set out for Cape Coast, our assigned destination.

What adventures lay ahead we could only conjecture. But withal, we looked forward to the challenges that we knew must be awaiting us.

4

Cape Coast, Our City

A city that is set on an hill cannot be hid. (Matthew 5:14)

The beauty and serenity of Cape Coast lay before us. A city with a population of around 60,000 and set on rolling hills, it overlooked the Gulf of Guinea, where the azure waters became one with the sky. A castle of ancient vintage brooded over the shoreline.

> Although it appears to have its share of poverty, with evidence of the same symptoms as Accra—crumbling and decaying buildings, many unfinished with rusting steel pointing skyward—Cape Coast is such a far cry from Accra as to seem almost a different world.
>
> Here in Ghana, as had been envisioned, are beautiful ocean beaches, tall palms, and tropical vegetation. Stately though run-down mansions perch on hilltops, reminiscent of Samoa, Fiji and Hawaii. Our spirits have soared since arrival. (*Journal.*)

Desire to see the chapel site brought us to one of our first stops. It is hard to imagine a more idyllic setting. In tranquility on the western outskirts of Cape Coast, it nestled at the junction of a palm-lined road along the gulf and a new bi-pass highway skirting the city. It also was near a main entrance to Cape Coast University, whose several-hundred-acre campus spread out over the undulating hills. Miles of stately palms lined the golden shoreline nearby where, tirelessly, curling waves thunderously boomed and hissed as they washed the sands of the wide and gently sloping beach.

On this grassy plot where goats now grazed and children scampered, we could easily visualize the first Latter-day Saint chapel that would be built in Ghana. We longed to begin without delay.

Our delight was further enhanced as with open arms our black brothers and sisters welcomed us. Among the first was Joseph William Billy Johnson, the almost legendary founder of Mormonism in Ghana. Already feeling at home, our hearts found responsive kinship.

Old Cape Coast chapel, exterior.

On the first Sabbath day, our first glance at the one-room warehouse-like building that for almost 20 years had served as a chapel for these humble people, revealed in graphic terms why a new one was needed. But even as they had, we learned to appreciate it as a place of true worship, a haven of rich spirituality despite lowly appearances.

Situated in an old, run-down, and crowded section of town near the castle, the building, about 30 by 50 feet, with walls of clay or cement once plastered smoothly, manifested obvious signs of decay. Crevices and holes in the uneven concrete floor not only kept footsteps cautious, they provided reservoirs for rain that found ready access through gaping holes in an ancient and rusting corrugated iron roof. Walls were cracked and the paint was chipped and peeling. Two glassless windows on one side, fitted with vertical iron bars and creaking shutters which sagged open, allowed light and air to filter in.

A large upright piano, no doubt a once beautifully ornate instrument but now warped and peeling, stood against one wall. Its yellowed and broken keys were silent, with wires and workings long since removed to serve perhaps in some important but less melodious project. Backless benches which served as pews, made from rough sawn lumber, now gleamed with the satin patina of long use. Among the benches a few rickety metal chairs found place.

But let me quickly add that this lowly room was not without beauty. On the wall behind the podium were painted three figures. The central and dominant one was of the Savior, larger than life size, with arms outspread, lovingly inviting all to "Come Unto Me," as was captioned above. His eyes of infinite sadness, yet love, drew mine to his like a magnet. On each side of him the Angel Moroni was depicted, trumpet raised to lips, proclaiming the good news.

Near the center of the room by a main pillar, supported on a base about three feet high and larger than life size, was a statue of Angel Moroni with trumpet raised to lips; feet resting on a ball. This magnificent work of art, crafted from concrete and painted creamy white, had as its only model the picture on the cover of a blue paperback copy of the Book of Mormon.

Primary class.

All this art work and sculpting, done long before the authority of the priesthood arrived in Ghana and without knowledge of customary LDS chapels, witnessed the love and devotion of these people for the Savior.

Angel Moroni.

This room became special to me. Without piano or other accompaniment, the singing was sweet and reverent. Classes convened back-to-back without any dividers, never disturbing each other's concentration: Relief Society; Elders Quorum; two classes of Primary children sitting attentively, softly singing at times or in quiet activities; Young Women; Aaronic Priesthood; and always a large class of investigators, filled the room with gentle sounds of worship.

> At Cape Coast First Branch meetings this A.M. dear little four-year-old Baba Acquah, head on my lap, proceeded to go to sleep. Such a darling. Perspiration beaded her face in the hot stuffy room. My small fan attempted to keep us both cool. As I sat listening to the sermons in Fante, my eyes and ears were irresistibly drawn to other sights and sounds: little goats bleating, neighbor children playing and shouting near the open door, shafts of sunlight streaming through holes in the roof, resting upon this one or that like a benediction, the wet floor and water-filled cracks telling of rain during the night, flies drawing attention to their antics, as in groups they flit around the floor or drone in lazy circles. Listening all the while, the lilting cadence of their language lends meaning to the words. I feel so happy among these dear people. (*Journal*, 27 November, 1983.)

Even curious chickens seemed almost at home, as at times during services one might, with some uncertainty, strut up the aisle, head bobbing this way and that. The almost street-level floor was easily accessible through doors swung wide at all times. Street children would shyly peek in to see what was going on. If near enough, I would beckon them in, but usually they fled.

But in this far off land, in this room with conditions most humble, I enjoyed some of the sweetest feelings of my life. I loved this room and the feelings I had while in it. And here where materialistic mores of the world had not corrupted, the Spirit seemed unrestrained.

I will always hold sacred a testimony received during sacramental service one Sunday while singing a hymn:

> There is a green hill far away,
> Without a city wall,
> Where the dear Lord was crucified,
> Who died to save us all.

We may not know, we cannot tell,
What pains he had to bear,
But we believe it was for us
He hung and suffered there.
(*Hymns,* p. 194.)

As we sang the last two lines of the second verse a great wave of warmth and ecstasy flooded my entire being. Tears sprang from my eyes as I felt wholly enveloped in the Savior's love for me and for all. I knew that he truly died to save us all if we will but accept his magnificent and supreme sacrifice and follow after him. This special feeling in that humble room will always remain with me. It confirmed that external surroundings are irrelevant to the Spirit.

Easter 1984, which began as any other Sabbath, became another memorable day:

> April 22, a beautiful Easter Sabbath. Absent were the materialistic displays of the holy celebration; no Easter bunnies, no colored eggs or candies, no Easter finery paraded—just reverent attitudes as they commemorated the atonement and resurrection of our Savior. All week throughout the city churches had been holding special services. Last week, Palm Sunday, palm branches were flourished as the various groups sang and paraded around the streets and church yards. In this area, predominantly Christian, religion is taken seriously and unashamedly.
>
> Cape Coast Second Branch meetings held first, were enjoyed with taped organ music (sent by one of our children). Echoing through the rafters, it sounded heavenly.
>
> First Branch meetings began promptly afterwards with classes first. Through glassless windows swirling black clouds menaced. During the opening hymn of sacrament meeting the wind set in fiercely. A cacophony of clattering and banging gained momentum as the loose edges of the ancient metal roof, riddled with holes, were whipped by the sharp gusts, hurling bits of rusty metal and debris in hair, on clothes, and throughout the room.
>
> Then the rains came. Lashed through holes in the roof, puddles began collecting on the floor. Most of us huddled on one side of the room where more shelter was found. Umbrellas went up.

Singing in the rain.

Amid the din of flapping roof metal, roaring wind, and pelting rain, the service continued, smiles unquenched.

The sacrament table, relocated to a more protected area, had cloths shaken and water cups refilled from our thermos in the car. Their supply was "finished." with no other fresh water available. The sacrament prayers rose above the tumult of nature.

A special feeling of love and dedication to our Savior permeated the meeting. Despite the uproar, discomforts and perhaps even hazards, no one left.

To be part of the spiritual outpouring this day was a privilege. Called out of the audience to speak on the atonement and resurrection of the Savior, I felt blessed beyond measure just to be counted worthy to be among these humble, exemplary servants of Christ. (*Journal.*)

This one-room chapel had indeed served long and well. What joy will fill the hearts of these saints when a beautiful chapel dedicated to the Lord will be among them. Every endeavor to insure the reality of this was our pledge.

5

Open Minds and Ready Hearts

For it shall come to pass in that day, that every man shall hear the fulness of the gospel in his own tongue, and in his own language, through those who are ordained unto this power,... (D & C 90:11)

Since that day in June 1983 when Elder David B. Haight, an apostle of the Lord Jesus Christ, dedicated the land of Ghana for the preaching of the gospel, this field in the Lord's vineyard has been growing by leaps and bounds.

Caught up in the excitement of teaching the gospel from the first day of arrival, we found people of all ages clamoring and virtually lining up to be taught. Since we hadn't received the chapel drawings as yet, our full time was devoted to teaching. This joy was noted early in an August 1983 letter to our children:

> They are so easy to teach; their spirits so willing. I think of the Savior's words, "My sheep hear my voice, and I know them, and they follow me." (John 10:27) They are ready, just waiting to be brought into the fold. Sunday—taught a group of 12 so eager they can hardly wait for baptism. Monday and Tuesday—taught classes to new ones and filled in some missing lessons for others. Wednesday—gave the final lesson to a group, now ready for baptism, depending on their interviews. After the beginning of today's class of 13, seven more joined the group, some new, others needing a few lessons. It's amazing how they flock in. A missionary could never desire a better situation.

Proselyting was unnecessary as friends brought friends, relatives brought relatives, and neighbors brought neighbors, who in turn brought others, providing a constant source of contacts. Without exception, group teaching was the norm. If classes began with few, the numbers always grew. This mandated accurate records to assure that each received all lessons, one of the requisites for baptism.

A new missionary couple, Leland and Marie Houseley, of Dallas, Texas, arrived on the 5th of August and were assigned to organize a branch at Kumasi. This brought the total to three missionary couples in Ghana. Due to government regulation, the entry of more couples into the country was limited. During our tenure that number was not increased.

At a district conference convened by President Cooper in Cape Coast on Saturday, August, 1983, the Cape Coast District was organized from the Accra District, which previously comprised all of Ghana. This division was essential due in part to the acute petrol shortage which severely curtailed travel.

At this same meeting the Cape Coast Branch was divided into two branches, as the small meeting place could no longer accommodate so many. This made a total of seven branches in the new district: Moree, Sofokrom, Mpintsin, Assin Foso, Takoradi, and two in Cape Coast.

The following day, at the Accra District conference, President Cooper divided the one Accra branch into three, which, with Tema, comprised the Accra District. Eleven branches were now thriving in Ghana, with another soon to be organized in Kumasi.

Another milestone at the Cape Coast conference was noted when four splendid young Ghanaians were called as Ghana's first district missionaries. It began the fulfillment for Ghana of the Savior's words that the gospel would be preached to all peoples in their own tongue. (D & C 90:11) Although English is the official language, many do not speak or understand it. This assistance to teach the growing numbers of investigators was a blessing, as our time became increasingly consumed in building the chapel and procurement of hard-to-find materials.

The four missionaries called were Andrew Imbrah, Kojo Amankwah, Edward Sagoe, and Emmanuel Gyamfi. The latter had been a member of the Church not quite two months. Brother Johnson, when called at this time to serve as supervisor over the district missionaries, was placed in a favorable position to continue his enthusiastic and effective missionary work.

When the difficult-to-obtain missionary lessons and teaching aids were finally received, our home became a "mini MTC," as we modestly called it. It was our privilege to be a part of the development of these humble men and, with the help of the Lord, guide them through the training we ourselves had so recently received.

With facility of mind and speech they soon mastered the materials for presentation and, with total commitment, put their lives into the hands of the Lord. This will always be a memorable occasion, as never have we seen young men more dedicated and able to learn by the Spirit than these. Becoming humble, diligent teachers, they brought many into the light of the gospel.

Where the native tongue was needed, these missionaries became more effective than we. But teaching through an interpreter continued to be a joy for us. Despite the language barrier, as candidates progressed and were invited to review their acceptance of Jesus Christ, Joseph Smith, and other principles, they left no doubt as to their feelings, even if spoken in Fante.

Although assistance in teaching was now available, Max remained solely responsible for all baptisms and interviews for such in the seven branches in Cape Coast District. This work had not as yet been given into the hands of the branch presidents. Max loved these interviews, where, even as in teaching, their spirits radiated the truths felt.

In Ghana polygamy is sanctioned by law, so early in their lessons it was necessary to ascertain the marital status of each man and woman being taught. Those practicing polygamy were not eligible for baptism, as to do so would violate Church policy. But even that problem was solved when true principles were understood. Precious souls were willing to sacrifice to come into the fold of Christ.

A touching story was related to us by a formerly polygamous family, a man with two wives who lived in a village near Nuamakrom. Converted to the gospel more than two years previous to our coming, they yearned for baptism. For some time they pondered how their lives could be brought into compliance with gospel standards. They knew the gospel was true, but without a change none of them would ever be able to partake of its blessings. Finally the first wife proposed that she divorce her husband, as the second wife had borne children, but she herself had not. This, they decided, was the only solution and was accomplished. Thus they had lived in harmony with Church standards for over a year.

It was Max's pleasure to interview these three faithful souls, finding them all worthy. They, along with 15 from Assin Foso, and with 14 from Nuamakrom who had walked more than eight miles through jungle trails to Assin Foso, were baptized in a shallow jungle stream.

The ocean, for coastal branches, provided the only water sufficient in quantity for baptisms, which required total immersion. This could occasion bits of unexpected hilarity. At the seashore of Moree, with no breakwater or rocks, waves came rolling and crashing with vigor from the vast expanse of the ocean. To negotiate these waves required watchful planning and sure-footedness for the officiators as well as the candidates. But in spite of all precautions, a large rolling wave might catch them off guard, to totally engulf the group and send them sprawling on the sand.

Another condition to monitor was to anticipate a swell of water high enough for immersion, which otherwise at ebbing would leave them high and dry. On many occasions repeated attempts were necessary, but in all instances, despite blinking and sputtering, all came up smiling.

A jungle baptism, also special, was not without its peculiar difficulties. Finding enough water in the few and sometimes almost dry streams presented a challenge, as noted 6 November, 1983 at Assin Foso, about 50 miles inland:

> The baptisms were held after the Sunday service which was greatly prolonged until Max, with the help of District President S.A. Kwaw and Brother J.W.B Johnson, had interviewed 32 candidates. During this meeting I was asked to speak (through an interpreter as always) and to take all the time I wanted. Max slyly joked later that this must have been the opportunity I had always longed for.
>
> Afterwards, most of the congregation gathered with us about a mile distant where a stream, shallow and root beer colored, meandered out of the deep shadows of the jungle growth. No crystal streams here, tumbling from snow capped peaks. The water, clear brown but not muddy, derived its color from the vegetation, and did not stain the white clothing. It brought to mind the poem, which as a child conjured such youthful imagery:

Dark brown is the river,
Golden is the sand.
It flows along forever
With trees on every hand.

Green leaves a-floating,
Castles of the foam.
Boats of mine a-boating,
Where will all come home?
(Robert Louis Stevenson,
A Child's Garden of Verses)

Through the growth of small rubber trees, bushes, towering mahoganies and tangled vines from which Tarzan could have swung happily, we picked our way to the selected spot. The 32 candidates dressed in white looked angelic as we assembled where the stream was deepest.

Due to shallowness of the water, barely mid-calf, the candidates sat on the stream bed, and were laid backward into the water. Generally it was necessary to hold their feet down. Such a gentle method of performing the ordinance.

Confirmation, also in a green cathedral of jungle trees, was a fitting climax to a spiritual day. (*Journal.*)

When all was completed, branch president J.K. Baako earnestly enquired, "When are you coming back to baptize 30 more? We have them ready."

Eight miles distant, in the village of Nuamakrom and in another village about four miles further on, lived a few members who were part of the Assin Foso branch. The only means of travel between there and Assin Foso was by footpath through the jungle, or on occasion by an ancient railroad of known unreliability. As everyone was not able to walk the eight to twelve miles to church on Sundays this group held meetings of their own, with President Baako's counselor, Brother George Cudjoe, who lived in that area, as head.

Of the 32 just baptized in Assin Foso, 17 had walked the eight miles and more. Here also lived the 30 others who were awaiting baptism. Some had paid tithing for more than two years, attesting to their faith. A patient people, the Ghanaians have taught us volumes. No roads reached into these remote villages, and we were told that no missionaries had as yet visited them. We determined to do so when possible.

Some three months later the trip into Nuamakrom was arranged. Brother Johnson, his son Brigham, and Elder Imbrah, went ahead days before to determine if Nuamakrom could be reached by a different route which would eliminate the long jungle trek or the uncertain train. While there they gathered the villagers together to teach and review gospel principles with them. Returning, they brought necessary directions. My Journal noted:

> 25 February, 1984. At dawn, the van packed with a foam twin mattress, linens, food, water, Church books, tape recorder, a sacramental service set, and a change of clothing, we set out for Nuamakrom, where with the help of Elders Johnson and Imbrah we will do the long awaited baptisms. The first 20 miles was on good hard-surfaced road, then 30 more on an orange dirt one, where in spite of closing all windows, choking dust billowed in and settled on us till upon arrival at Twifo Prosso we looked like orange clowns. Leaving our sleeping gear there, we then bumped along for seven miles on a single track road, plowing through nearly impenetrable jungle, with trees brushing on either side; exotic birds squawking and monkeys chattering.
>
> Anticipating our arrival, the villagers had widened the foot path with their cutlasses for about the last mile so the van could pass through. The gullies and washouts along the trail, so deep that wheels could drop out of sight, caused grave apprehension and careful maneuvering. Finally, a deep ravine with the bridge washed out brought us to a halt. Met there by porters, our books, briefcases and other equipment were put on their heads.(They usually never let us carry anything, not even my purse.) One man remained to guard the van.
>
> At Nuamakrom, after a steamy 15-minute walk through the bush, we were met by a crowd of eagerly awaiting baptismal candidates. Already 11 a.m., interviews began immediately with Max and Brother Johnson, interpreter, sitting in the shade of a baobab tree. Again they found interviews to be slow and painstaking, due not only to the language barrier but also to a lack of record keeping, making birth and marriage dates laborious

to recall. Family names many times are not carried on, as each child may be given a different surname.

Although the 40 interviews were not completed, it was essential that we traverse the treacherous roads to our sleeping quarters before dark. Promising to be back by 8 a.m., we returned to our van, again accompanied by the porters with all our equipment on their heads.

Traveled eight miles back to Twifo Prosso, where thanks to Brother Johnson's arrangement we were lodged in a nurses' cottage near the hospital. There, without electricity or running water, we enjoyed their hospitality. After refreshing ourselves with cool baths from a bucket of water placed in the shower room by our hostess, we slept peacefully, with not a mosquito to disturb us.

Meeting again at the ravine Sunday morning, and leaving a guard as before, the porters aided our return to Nuamakrom. Interviews finally completed, all trooped to a nearby shallow, brown, jungle creek for the baptism of 42. Then back to the schoolroom where confirmations and ordinations to the appropriate Aaronic Priesthood office were performed.

Sacrament meeting followed. The new priesthood holders were instructed on how to perform the ordinance of the sacrament of the Lord's Supper, and did so humbly and well. Twenty babies and small children were given blessings, followed by more Aaronic Priesthood ordinations of those we had baptized last November.

Nuamakrom was the nucleus of a cluster of smaller villages which radiated like the spokes of a wheel into the surrounding jungle. Most of those just baptized lived in one of these outlying villages, which was even more difficult to reach than Nuamakrom. Brother Cudjoe, the priesthood leader and a member for several years, was one of these and had helped prepare many of his village for baptism. He had built a chapel in his village so that they would have a place to meet. Intrigued, we desired to see this jungle chapel.

Although exhausted in the heat by the time the meetings were concluded at 2 o'clock, we nevertheless decided that some of our group should visit this chapel. When asked how far it was they replied "35 minutes." Distance is measured by time, not miles. Deciding there was time enough to go to this village and still return home before dark, Max and Brother Johnson set off. Max describes this journey:

Brother Cudjoe, our guide, promptly set out on a wide and well defined trail. After a few minutes, however, it narrowed, requiring us to walk single file. A tall, slender man, obviously accustomed to such activity, Brother Cudjoe set a brisk pace which Brother Johnson had no problem maintaining, but one which I found quite taxing.

During this fast walk our guide never once paused to rest, nor even looked back to see if we were still coming. Although able to keep up, at times I had to push hard just to keep him in sight. This was important, because a number of trails branched off, with little or no indication as to where they led. We passed other villages along the way, attested to by the various sounds reaching our ears, but dense vegetation hid everything from view. Other sounds of monkeys and various birds, as well as small ground animals, all contributed to the jungle cadence.

At times a large log was across the path. Simple—jump over it. After all, this was a foot path and who had even a small motor bike? One log conveniently spanned a small ravine, to serve as a bridge.

With a sense of accomplishment, almost exactly 35 minutes after starting, we stepped into a clearing containing a small cluster

Jungle chapel.

of buildings. We had arrived. The village consisted of perhaps 12 or 15 mud and bamboo huts, arranged in an informal circle around an open space which was far from level, one side being considerably higher than the rest. The object of our quest, immediately apparent, was the largest and most prominent building in the cluster. Located on the highest ground, the chapel, by far the most skillfully constructed, commanded a view of the surrounding buildings.

Without measuring, I judged its size to be about 16 by 30 feet. Built of mud and bamboo, it had a thatched roof, the same as all other buildings in the village. However, the walls, both inside and out, were cement plastered, with doors in one side and end. Glassless windows and open gable ends provided ample light and ventilation. Inside, the dirt floor was smoothly packed, with a platform two steps high built across one end. Furnishings consisted only of wooden benches.

Although not the least pretentious, judged by contemporary standards (the rest of the village) it was a magnificent structure, built principally by one dedicated brother, at his own expense. Although most of the building materials were available locally, (mud, bamboo, palm fronds, etc.) some items had to be brought in the hard way—on heads. A sack of cement for plaster could well cost a month's wages, to say nothing of the effort involved to carry it the 3 1/2 miles from Nuamakrom. Such dedication continues to thrill us.

Though the day had been long and the walk tiring, I felt such an exhilaration and renewal of both body and spirit that I barely noticed the 35 minute walk back to Nuamakrom.

Accompanied by two sisters with generous gifts of ten eggs, a large stalk of bananas, and sugar cane for our refreshment, we returned to the van, aided by porters and many of our new brothers and sisters. The brother guarding the van, slated to be ordained, was jubilant as Max and Brother Johnson performed the ordinance, thus concluding a full rich day. What a glorious time! As so often, we could not refrain from exclaiming, "How can you top this?"

The return home was cooler and dust-free following a refreshing rain. Truly, this was a never-to-be-forgotten experience!

Group awaiting baptism.

On the beach at Sekondi, one baptismal service for the Takoradi Branch held joy for many, but for one little girl, disappointment. There were no upsets as the breakwater of one of Ghana's principal ports kept the water calm and peaceful. All 20 in turn came out of the water happy and smiling. But one small girl in white, who had been dancing with expectancy all the while, looked sad and downcast when at the end her name had not been called to be baptized. Investigation revealed she had not reached the age of eight but, having attended Primary with the other children preparing for baptism, assumed she would also be done. Given a comfort blessing, she felt content when assured that her time would come.

Even confirmations after baptism became unpredictable when dealing with the ocean, as on one occasion at Cape Coast. The confirming of over 30 was performed at the beach on a rock padded with plastic cushions. When begun the tide was far down the beach, but by completion water was swirling mid-calf around their legs.

One older woman, after her confirmation at this service, related to me that as hands were laid upon her head, while her eyes were closed, a bright light appeared before her eyes, which was to her a testimony that she had made the right choice.

The opportunity for converts was everywhere, at any time:

> To Komenda to teach Margaret Appiah her last discussion. She desired baptism with the group on Saturday. During her lunch hour at the post office, chairs positioned under the spreading mango tree offered welcome relief from the sun. As we began the lesson, a fellow postal employee stood on one side of Margaret, showing great interest as he read the scriptural references with her. Soon another curious friend, listening intently, flanked the other side. As the lesson progressed the presence of the Holy Spirit was apparent and which, I perceived, Margaret was also aware. "Wherefore, he that preacheth and he that receiveth, understand one another and both are edified and rejoice together." (D & C 50:22) This depicts so clearly how we felt so frequently. (*Journal.*)

These two postal workers, also touched by the Spirit, were later baptized, along with three other men from Komenda.

Margaret's baptismal service was to us another notable first:

> At 2 p.m. a group assembled where the first ordinances on the Church property were performed. Ten baptisms initiated the new water tank as a temporary font. Primarily intended for water storage, it doubled nicely for our purposes. Built of concrete block and plastered smoothly on the inside, it was ten feet square and three feet deep. Margaret Appiah, baptized first, was followed by the other nine in quick succession. How simple to baptize in quiet water, compared to the turbulence of the ocean or the scarcity in the jungle streams. A lovely occasion, with the meeting held under the palm-thatched bower of the construction shack. (*Journal*, 11 February, 1984.)

Each baptismal service, under the direction of a branch presidency, was well organized. Lines would form as the branch clerk gave each a slip of paper whereon their full name was written. This was essential to insure accuracy, such as when the large group was baptized at the Sekondi beach on New Year's Eve day, 1983:

> What a glorious culmination to a year! With President Kwaw and Brother Johnson accompanying us, we left at daylight for Sofokrom. (No earlier due to the curfew.) There, Max and the

> brethren personally interviewed 31 candidates for baptism. During this time I reviewed the lessons with those awaiting interviews and challenged them with gospel questions. Strength and potential leadership were exhibited by so many.
>
> On to Mpintsin where 28 more were awaiting interviews. How the Lord is directing his children was revealed by an experience one of the candidates, Thomas A. Arthur, shared with me:
>
> "While searching for a church to join, I had a vivid dream in which a man appeared. Showing me three large letters—LDS—he said that I should join that church as it is the true church. The dream ended but I was puzzled, not knowing what LDS meant or stood for. The next day at work in my railroad office, seeing a fellow worker reading a book, I asked what he was reading. Replying that it was the Book of Mormon, he added that it was a book from the LDS Church. I asked what the letters meant. Upon hearing 'The Church of Jesus Christ of Latter-day Saints,' I replied that I must join that church as it is the true church. Could he tell me where to find it? No, he could not. Someone had given him the book and he knew nothing about the church.
>
> "Being almost obsessed with the desire to find the Church, I quit my job and started searching. One day, while walking on a rural road, I noticed a weathered sign about four feet square bearing the name of the Church. A directional arrow pointed to a steep and deeply rutted road leading to Mpintsin. (A small village atop the hill) I at once set out in the direction indicated. Asking the first man I met if he knew any LDS people, he informed me that he himself was one and, yes, I could be taught about the Church."
>
> Mr. Arthur soon joined the investigators class that Elder Edward Sagoe, a district missionary, was teaching in Mpintsin, and was now among the 28 being interviewed for baptism. He expressed great joy in finding the Church.

On our next visit to Mpintsin, Brother Arthur was there to greet us, veritably glowing. Even though as yet he held no position in the branch he was busy straightening benches, helping children, and welcoming all with an outpouring of love. I was so impressed by this sweet man; but then we never ceased to be amazed at the wonders we witnessed.

The Journal entry for 31 December, 1983 continues:

> At Takoradi five more candidates were interviewed, following which all assembled at Sekondi beach where the baptisms were performed. What a marvelous group! I'm sure the Lord is pleased this day. All 64 newly baptized members posed for an historic photo, this being the largest group we were privileged to baptize to date. We would have preferred all to be dressed in white but this was not possible as sufficient white clothing was not available. Several people shared the same clothes, with eager candidates quickly pulling on wet garments just used by another, some sets of clothing being used several times in quick succession. From all walks of life they came, men and women, young and old, some poor, some educated and influential.
>
> Despite the heat and the long strenuous day of interviews, baptisms, and confirmations, upon arriving home, instead of fatigue, we feel exhilaration. "How can you top this?" This must be experienced to believe. Indeed the harvest is golden as the field is garnered.

And so it continued, with baptisms nearly every week in one or another of the branches in the district. Always spiritual events, these services invoked loving support from branch members. We praise the district missionaries who helped us in teaching.

Mission guidelines wisely provided that no one be baptized without first completing the prescribed course of lessons, nor anyone who was under the age of 18 unless another Church member of that age or older was in the household to lend support. This second requirement brought an interesting development in one instance.

Teaching in groups, as was usual, it was possible at times to be unaware of all the facts about each person being taught. Faustina, 13 years old, received all the lessons and desired baptism. At her interview, however, all were disappointed to learn that she would be the only member in her family and so did not meet the specified requirements. After explaining to her that she must have an "older" member in her home, again she came, bringing an older brother for the next course of lessons. He likewise readily accepted the teachings, but again she was thwarted, as in the interview it was learned that the brother, who looked much older, was only 15.

Undaunted, she came for a third set of discussions, this time bringing her father. This little angel was jubilant when soon thereafter all three were baptized. "And a little child shall lead them." (2 Nephi 21:6)

President Cooper reported that the brethren in Salt Lake City had expressed concern over the growing number of persons being baptized, fearing that they may not become sufficiently integrated or that the leaders could not properly minister to them. He commented, "That's a problem for which any mission president in the world would give his eye teeth."

We understood this concern. Care was observed to baptize only those who would be under the strong leadership of existing organizations as we knew that strength must come from strength. Many were joining the fold, but all would be under established, capable leadership.

For the stability of the Church as well as family life, the trend of baptisms was favorably noted in a letter to our children:

> One amazing and wonderful thing here, almost phenomenal from what seems to be the usual, is that men are in the forefront in accepting the gospel. They eagerly grasp their potential to become leaders. In Moree, where leadership was desperately needed after the branch president moved away, the Lord prepared and called a man, Theophilus Pratt, to take over the reins of the branch presidency just one month after his baptism. He became a strong spiritual leader. Likewise in Takoradi where Charles Bessa-Simons, whom we baptized just a few months ago, is now a strong branch president. Both of their families were brought into the Church soon after their (the fathers') own baptisms.

Another example of strong educated leadership is Andrew Coleman of the Admissions Department at Cape Coast University, who heard about the gospel through Banyan Dadson, then Dean of the University and head of the Chemistry Department. His testimony at district conference, 15 January, 1984, was noted in my journal:

> Brother Coleman, taught by the district missionaries, was still troubled by his three-pack-a-day smoking habit. During his baptismal interview with Max and his branch president, Holdbrooke MacArthur, he was asked if he had given up smoking. After answering no, he promised he would do so as soon as he was baptized. Three times the question was searchingly asked:

"Are you sure you will give up smoking when baptized?" and each time he answered with firm conviction that he had committed himself to quit. The decision was made, aided by the Spirit, to proceed with his baptism.

As he was being immersed in the waters of baptism, Brother Coleman testified, he felt a change go over his body, and never since that day, the 8th of October 1983, some 2 1/2 months ago, has he desired a cigarette.

On November 28th Brother Coleman baptized his lovely wife and five of his children. Soon he was in a position of responsibility as clerk of the Cape Coast District. Since our return home Brother Coleman has been to England for job training and while there received his temple blessings. Many others whom we baptized are emerging as leaders, all anxiously engaged in building up the kingdom of God. How truly rewarding it is to witness the progress.

To baptize entire villages would perhaps have been easy. One tribal chief, who had attended some of our classes, invited us to his village, to which he escorted us December 11th:

Accompanied by Brother Johnson, we met the chief of several villages at Kissi, where we were to take him to his main village to explain the basic doctrines of the Church. The chief, who spoke English, directed the way. Driving seven miles into the bush over deeply rutted and gully-washed roads, untouched by road grader, proved rather hazardous.

Upon arrival, the chief's gong was sounded to call all the villagers together. Under a palm-thatched shelter, or abe ase, the chief, thoroughly looking the part, seated himself on his "Ashanti stool," the symbol of authority. Max and I, seated in arm chairs, with a few others on chairs around the perimeter of the shelter, were surrounded by a sea of men, women, and children, whose intense eyes studied our every movement.

After a brief conversation in Fante, presumably with his tribal leaders, the chief asked Max to tell them about the Church. With Brother Johnson interpreting, Max explained that we represented the Lord Jesus Christ and were there to teach them the doctrines that are for the benefit and happiness of all God's children. After

> explaining many gospel truths, he told about Joseph Smith and his part in the restoration of the gospel of Jesus Christ.
>
> The message was well received by the chief and the villagers who, seated on the ground, had gradually crept closer as though a drawstring had gathered them in. I felt comfortable and secure. I was delighted when, afterwards, several timidly approached me to try out their halting English.
>
> The visit was enjoyable, but it was getting late, and as always, treacherous roads must be traveled in daylight. Upon leaving, gifts of coconuts and oranges appeared as if by magic. (*Journal.*)

A few days later the chief again expressed gratitude for our visit to his village and added, "They will all join." However, with the press of building and teaching we were never able to return to that remote village, but there awaits a golden harvest when conditions are right and trained leaders are available.

In a class at Assin Foso, typically, various ages and personalities were represented:

> We taught the four class members through an interpreter. Each was invited to relate what he knew and felt about Joseph Smith. Although spoken in Fante, the sparkle in the eyes of two 13-year-old boys, and the fervor of their testimonies, brought tears to our eyes. One married woman of evident wealth and education bore a sweet testimony of Joseph Smith, adding, "This is so beautiful. It's just what I've been looking for. It's so logical."
>
> But my heart was extremely touched by a demure 15-year-old girl who shyly, with head bent to one side, when asked why she desired to join the Church, responded, "The Lord has done so much for me and I want to belong to his true church." She did not go to school, nor could she read or write, but the Lord had spoken to her soul, she said. I felt her sweet, tender spirit. She is perhaps someone's maid, as generally they do not attend school, which is a pity. (*Journal.*)

Our building site security guard, Anthony McCarthy, a kindly but disciplined, straight-as-a-ramrod retired army sergeant, loved reading the Book of Mormon, and did so diligently from the time he began his gospel instruction. His reply to a friend who desired to borrow the book, "Oh no! I can't part with it. I read it every day," showed his love and commitment to it.

Shortly before baptism he requested a Doctrine and Covenants, which I supplied him. A few days later, when asked if he were reading the book, he replied in lyrical terms, "Oh yes, Madam, (accent on the last syllable) I'm enjoying it very much. It's very fine. It's so sweet to my taste, just like eating sweet and delicious fruit. It makes me feel so happy."

"Sarg," I replied, (he loved my nickname for him) "You have quoted some of the very words in Lehi's dream about the tree of life, and of partaking of its fruit that was delicious to the taste, having the power to make one happy." (See 1 Nephi 8). He was pleased with my comment as was I to have him so eloquently describe the joys of the gospel.

Funerals often afford opportunities to present gospel messages. This held true in Ghana:

> Elizabeth Mensah, whom we baptized in August, died January 16th. Tonight was her wake-keeping, a traditional pre-funeral ceremony. Ordinarily the affair is boisterous, with drum beating, clapping, singing, and dancing, but, at least during the time we were there, it was a peaceful and reverent meeting with perhaps 200 friends gathered to bid her farewell.
>
> Although the wake began at 6 p.m., we along with Brother Johnson did not arrive until some time later. Many hymns were sung. At times weeping and wailing rose in crescendos from the women mourners in the room with the coffin, away from our view. The congregation, seated on benches in a backyard compound, found the air stifling with not a hint of breeze reaching the enclosure.
>
> Without prearrangement, Max was invited to speak about Church doctrines to those assembled, most of whom did not belong to the Church. During his talk the mourning at times became pervasive and shrill, but Brother Johnson, in his powerful voice, interpreted for all to hear.
>
> About 9 o'clock the power went off, thrusting us into total darkness, but Max continued for some time. After more hymns and a prayer we took our leave. (*Journal.*)

As a result of this event one elderly woman received a testimony of the truthfulness of Max's words, was taught and baptized.

The intelligent, spiritual men and women whom we baptized, capable of leadership, were a continual source of joy. Almost without exception they desired to serve in some manner. Each eligible male was ordained to the appropriate Aaronic Priesthood office soon after baptism and confirmation and was promptly oriented to his duties regarding the ordinance of the Sacrament of the Lord's Supper. The humble attitude of these men, of varying ages, as they proudly discharged sacred duties, was gratifying to observe.

What a power for good is developing in West Africa. To be a part of this spiritual upsurge, to see the growth and development of God's children in this nether part of his vineyard, is most rewarding. Assisted by the district missionaries, 374 souls were added to our district through the waters of baptism during our eleven months in Ghana.

An old saying, "A mind is not a vessel to be filled, but a lamp to be lit" never had more meaning than here where the light of the gospel is shining forth in ever-increasing brilliance.

6

Dearth of the Land

And the years of dearth began to come...and the dearth was in all the lands...and the famine waxed sore in the land.
(Genesis 41:54, 56)

This is an age-old problem in Africa, but now there was no Joseph inspired of the Lord to store food to feed the hungry in time of famine. Not only afflicted with drought, Ghana has all the attendant problems.

The "World Vision" publication for August-September 1984 related conditions very succinctly:

> Visit Ghana today and you'd be struck by the lack of water, the lack of electricity, the severe shortage of food even in a big city, the long lines of cars and trucks waiting fuel (10 days wait for 7 1/2 gal.), the high prices (a day's wages for a loaf of bread), the abandoned (unfinished) buildings and the shaky security.
>
> Ghana is one of at least eight African nations in immediate danger of total social and economic collapse. The entire continent of Africa is in serious trouble.

These conditions have been brought about by a multiplicity of reasons, the main one being a severe drought that has plagued a good share of the African continent. Two broad bands of drought stretch across Africa: through the midsection of the upper continent and across the midsection of the lower half of the continent. This has brought death by starvation or hunger-related diseases to millions. Climatologists claim that this long-pervading malady actually began in 1968 and over the subsequent years has worsened.

We found the people hungry. Many were lethargic. Children with distended bellies, spindly arms and legs, and thin orange hair, telltale evidence of kwashiorkor, the disease of protein deficiency, were common. In the Ga language of Africa the word means "the disease the first child gets when the second is on the way" and refers to the fact that the child who no longer is breast fed falls prey to this terrible affliction. Usually it occurs in children from four months to five years of age, after being weaned. Quoting again from my August 1983 letter:

> Today, in our class, a sweet mother had a perhaps year-old child wrapped on her back. How pitifully thin and listless it looked, with thin orange hair. When the child whimpered he was nursed from flabby, empty-looking breasts, changing from one to the other, hoping to coax a little nourishment from them.

Many adults showed similar conditions. On the streets some might ask for food, but never did we hear complaints. Our hearts went out to them for their endurance and long-suffering.

"Summertime, And the Livin' Is Easy," as an old tune so happily chants, does not apply here. Summertime, yes, always, but the livin' is not easy!

Brown, shrivelled cornstalks rustling in the searing sun bore mute evidence of once hopeful crops; some survived on a limited basis in sheltered, low-lying areas. Small fields of rice in these swampy areas were noted. The reservoir of the Volta River Hydroelectric Project was almost empty, forcing the power plant to operate on an intermittent schedule. Domestic water was also shut off at most inopportune times, either from lack of water or electricity to pump it.

In towns and villages the water supply was a constant problem. Many homes had no running water, except, as we quipped, when someone ran with a bucketful on their head. Around Cape Coast and other larger towns, outside pumps and faucets were strategically located for those who had no water piped into their homes. At times one would see a long line of pans, buckets, or similar receptacles, waiting to be filled. If water was "finished" the owners might be out of sight, but once the supply returned they would suddenly materialize and fill their containers. Then, with them balanced on heads and with perhaps a pail in each hand, they gratefully carried the water to their homes.

Children with water.

Even small children were expected to contribute their share in fetching water. Some loads, always carried on heads, appeared as heavy as the carriers. In the ever-present heat the sloshing or dripping of leaky pans or buckets must have been a welcome refreshment to those beneath. Many children became drenched and seemed to enjoy it.

When water supplies in town were shut off for some time, the pilgrimage was on; schools might even be dismissed to allow children to carry water. For miles the roads would be lined with people with pails or pans on heads, some going, some coming, from a little swamp or stream somewhere off in the bush. To find the source one only needed to follow a well-beaten path. If too flat a pan were used, leafy branches floating on top of the water would help control the sloshing.

Branches had other practical uses. Having no flares or warning signals for traffic problems, branches strewn along the highway presaged trouble. Always available, they were effective.

Seeing signs, "Save our Hospitals from Collapse," we soon discovered the hospital system was indeed in jeopardy and needed rescuing. With few medicines, linens, and little food, it was incumbent that patients furnish their own, if such could be obtained. Relatives or friends cooked the patient's food over open fires in the courtyard.

Piteously maimed and crippled adults and children hunched along the streets. Due to so few medical people, the necessary treatment is not available. The ratio of doctors in Ghana is desperately low, with many thousands of people to one doctor. Traditional methods of treatment and cures, using herbs and incantations, have their place, but also their limitations. A leper colony, housed in barracks-like buildings and cottages, was located on the western outskirts of Cape Coast.

Obtaining food was a constant challenge for most. Food was always in short supply and much of it low in nutritive value. Prices inflated beyond the average person's purse were a real cause for alarm and suffering. Most were fortunate if they had one meal a day. An excerpt from a letter in August 1983, to our children, depicted our feelings:

> Rain is desperately needed as crops are parched and burning. Famine is stalking the land. Each day hungry people knock on our door asking for food, some bearing pathetic notes of starvation. I cannot turn them away empty handed; a cup or two of rice or beans sends them away happy indeed.
>
> Two little boys, so thin and frail, come here often. I fix them a bowl of rice with butter, a hard-cooked egg, or beans if I have

some cooked, which they eat while sitting on the porch. Then they leave with a little bag of beans or corn to take to their grandmother who cares for them. It's a heart-rending situation.

Yesterday while I was parked in town, a beggar woman shuffled along with a thin listless baby wrapped on her back; a fragile little boy clutching her hand limped beside her. Stopping at the car she said nothing, but with a little moan looked at me with big hollow eyes. The bill I slipped into her hand was such a little bit. I wish it were more.

Before coming here, appeals on TV to help Africa had wrenched my heart and brought response. Now here I am in real life seeing it for myself. I feel I can't turn my back on any little thing I can do, as the Savior's words keep shouting in my ears: "Inasmuch as ye have done it unto the least of these my brethren, ye have done it unto me," (Matt. 25:40) and yet I feel so helpless. There's so little I can do.

And from another letter about this same time:

All you grandchildren be thankful for every bite of lovely food you have. Don't waste any. I see these frail, malnourished youngsters who could make many meals out of what you throw in the garbage pail, and they would be happy for it. While walking among the sidewalk shop tables one day, I paused to observe a child of about three years picking through the dry dirt and sand. Finding some small fish bones, she quickly put them in her mouth and chewed them up. Your heart fairly breaks to know they are actually starving before your eyes.

Having read how delicious Ghanaian bread was, we hoped we would not leave without experiencing that pleasure. My journal noted:

The people of Ghana have had no bread for about six months or more. Flour is now beginning to trickle in from France so bakers will soon be making bread again. Henrietta Dadson, a good friend and Church member, who is a baker, will let me know when she has some.

We were not disappointed as her bread was delicious. Only professional bakers, no housewives, were allowed to obtain flour at that time. They were required to make a specified number of loaves per sack of flour, and to sell them for a fixed price. A loaf, weighing about a pound, sold for 50 cedis, which is a usual day's wage, while a roll or biscuit was 10 cedis. Examples of other prices were: one egg or one small onion was 10, five tomatoes cost 20, a watermelon was about 350, and one cedi for a tangerine. Staying alive was a daily challenge. The official exchange rate was about 40 cedis to a U.S. dollar.

Mere words of thanks will never suffice to express the gratitude we feel for our Church leaders as they, with generosity and compassion, administer the welfare program of the Church. What a glorious principle this is, that reaches out and blesses the lives of thousands, yes millions, who through no fault of their own do not have enough food to sustain life. Such was the situation in Ghana.

Having become aware of the desperate plight, the Church sent two large shipments of food from Welfare Square in Salt Lake City. The first shipment of many tons was distributed several months before our arrival and a similar one shortly after. In each case a sizable portion was made available to Ghanaian relief agencies, as well as to members of the Church through their branch presidents.

From the shipment that arrived soon after our arrival each baptized member received an 80-lb. box containing 20 lbs. rice, 20 lbs. dry corn, 10 lbs. dry beans, 4 qts. cooking oil, 5 lbs. sugar, 5 lbs. powdered milk, and salt. These were foods to which they were accustomed and were a welcome supplement to available foods.

It was gratifying to observe the sisters joyfully collect their boxes of food. With public transportation being almost non-existent, a box, too heavy for a sister to lift onto her head by herself, was, with the help of others positioned thereon and then proudly carried home, sometimes a distance of several miles.

Included in the shipment was a year's supply of food for us three missionary couples serving in Ghana, as well as for President and Sister Cooper who spent half of their time in Ghana. It was our privilege to purchase this food from the Church, as if from a supermarket. Indeed, one had been provided.

As a result of this generous gift from our Heavenly Father's storehouse, we observed the thin hollow cheeks of both children and adults begin to fill out and energies rise. All who participate so unselfishly in this inspired program may take satisfaction and joy in knowing their efforts have brought blessings and hope into the lives of their far off brothers and sisters caught in the terrible drama of survival. Again the words of the Savior, "Inasmuch as ye have done it unto one of the least of these" so aptly apply.

How grateful we were for the variety of foods provided for us. With every bite of beef stew, instant potatoes, flour, corn, peas, beans, peaches, tuna, rice, Spam (enjoyed often and still loved) raisins, macaroni, and the many other wonderful products, we blessed the hands and hearts that had so lovingly prepared them.

An excerpt from a letter written in August, 1983 to our children contains this observation:

> I baked some bread today. My, it was lovely, but I feel almost guilty having it because Ghana has no bread. Some yeast was sent, but I must conserve, so I made a sour-dough starter. It worked well. Each time I open a can of food I thank the Lord for it. It all tastes so delicious, the beef stew is just like homemade. I don't know how we could survive without this help.

Few fresh vegetables to which we were accustomed, except onions and tomatoes, were available. Cabbage, seen on rare occasions, was promptly purchased. Lettuce and carrots, enjoyed perhaps twice during the year, were found in Accra, never in Cape Coast.

The powdered milk and chocolate drink sent by the Church, packed in plastic-lined boxes and so delicious at first, rapidly deteriorated in the hot, humid climate, becoming caked and spoiled. Milk was rarely obtainable on the market, and then only in expensive 5 oz. cartons. However, in Accra at the "Foreign Exchange " store, where only foreign currency was accepted, we found (one time only) some "long-life" milk, which will keep for many months without refrigeration, even in this climate. We were introduced to this kind in Samoa; here we also found it delicious. The cost, which ordinarily would have seemed prohibitive (the small bottles figured out $8.80 a gallon), we gladly paid for the small quantity found.

Finding a box of Kellogg's Corn Flakes, we were elated, but the thrill was short lived, as when eaten they were so tough and gummy they stuck to our teeth. Again the humidity had thwarted us. Other prized purchases at this store were some long-sought mayonnaise, Hellman's 8 oz. for $2.00; a can of soft drink, 70 cents; a pint tub of margarine, $1.70; and 4 hamburger patties, $2.80.

The scarcity of milk literally brought men to their knees, as on the ship docks at Tema they would lick up spilled powdered milk. Surprisingly, we saw no powdered milk to purchase. Some children live many years, perhaps their entire lives, without tasting milk other than from their mother's breast, which is the reason many are nursed for several years.

Every kernel of spilled grain was carefully picked up from the loading docks. Children meticulously scraped, dug out and ate any last vestiges of food that remained in a pot of porridge. Nothing was wasted. We counted our blessings over and over, and felt saddened for the wastefulness in America.

The bare, almost vacant shelves of a market, which we might compare to a "Safeway," were sad evidence of once prosperous days. Token items placed here and there made a brave showing.

Just prior to our arrival, about a quarter-million Ghanaian workers had been expelled from Nigeria to ease that country's economic woes. Their return put a strain on Ghana's economy which was also struggling for survival, but many were ingenious in creating jobs to make a few cedis. Some picked rocks (gravel) from dirt banks along roadways or gully washes, carrying them in baskets on their heads to dump in collection piles, where for a pittance they sold the gravel to contractors. As clay soil contains few pebbles, this is tedious work. Many sold bundles of sticks for firewood, homemade soap, glazed and painted clay beads, and any other items they could make.

In contrast to our children's and grandchildren's rooms with shelves and closets crammed with clothes and "things" that more than fulfill every need or dream, possessions or toys here are meager indeed. My journal noted:

> Sitting in the car while Max procured materials, I observed two little girls busily playing house, as is their wont all over the world. A rag draped over an old rusty wire frame made a doll bed. Two sticks were dolls, which they covered with another rag. Rusty tin cans were pots or dishes in which they stirred something with more sticks. No lawn or yard for playground, just some old

broken concrete steps by the street, but happy and contented they played.

A few imaginative boys proudly displayed toy cars and trucks made from tin cans and other scraps. Hoops rolled with T sticks were popular, which I as a youngster also enjoyed. Another hoop game or toy was rather ingenious. As the hoop rolled, a hand-held cord attached to the hoop would be given a tug at just the right moment. This controlled the speed of the hoop, rather like a yo-yo. But generally, there was little time to play as children were busy doing necessary chores.

The few cows observed, bony and emaciated, seemed to barely survive on the grazing from nutritionally-starved soils.

With the Ghanaians' love for cleanliness, they bathe and wash clothes often, making soap a much-needed item. All soap I observed was the homemade variety and must have been excellent as attested by the clean white clothes. Irregularly cut chunks of tan-colored soap in trays, balanced on heads of vendors or displayed on shop tables, were to be found almost everywhere. As for ourselves, the bars of hand soap brought from home were dwindling and soon we too would be using the homemade variety. Just in time Max proudly presented me with two bars purchased at the Foreign Exchange in Accra.

Waste water from a soap factory in Cape Coast must have been soapy, for on days when it flowed the banks of the small sludgy stream would be lined with women, either washing clothes or dipping up the liquid to carry home. We never, however, saw soap from this factory in the markets.

Toothbrushes or toothpaste likewise were not found, but nature had provided perhaps a better alternative, as most Ghanaians have strong, white teeth. On shop tables we observed small bundles of wooden sticks about four inches long and several times the thickness of wooden matches, and in answer to our query were told they were to clean the teeth. These sticks, split from wood naturally impregnated with a medicinal property, promote healthy teeth and gums. People were frequently seen chewing them as they walked, especially on their way to work in the mornings.

Obtaining petrol was a time-consuming problem for anyone with a car. The heavy four-wheel-drive V8 gas-guzzling Range Rover which we drove at first compounded the challenge. Soon after arrival I noted in my journal:

> Went hunting for petrol without results. Cars queued in lines are left for days, but always with someone guarding them. Rations cut from 10 to 5 gallons a week, but even so, none found anywhere this week.

In Accra supplies were no better, as necessary trips there were often extended while days were consumed in searching and waiting for enough petrol to return the 100 miles to Cape Coast. Regarding this ongoing problem my journal again stated:

> Still no petrol so we walked nearly two miles to the Adisadel post office to mail some letters, only to find they had no stamps. Yes, the dearth reaches into all facets of life. I know this work will go forward. For some reason we are in a holding pattern, but the Lord is over all and his work will not fail. If we are faithful and do all we can, problems will be overcome, I know.

Many times the Lord seemed to intervene. Daniel, our good friend and helper, on the lookout for petrol all week, met us as we drove to a station where we hoped to obtain some. He told us to drive directly into the station.

Although vehicles were lined up for blocks, they waved us in and put 10 gallons in the tank. The name of the Church with "Missionary" printed on the doors seemed to favor us many times.

Some of the Lord's faithful servants also helped in this dire need. Brother Johnson sometimes obtained petrol when we couldn't. (He lived beside a service station.) Coming to our home on occasion, he would drain all the petrol from his car and pour it into our tank stating, "There's enough in the carburetor to get home." What a generous, considerate friend, always willing to give anything he had.

Hiking to near assignments was necessary at times:

> Almost out of petrol, so will save it to go to Moree on Sunday. Loaded with books, posters and briefcase, we set out for Mfantsipim school where the Branch President's Training Seminar was held. After walking the 1 1/2 miles of ever-changing terrain, uphill and down, through tall grass, over rivulets in gullies, and across the school's soccer field, availing ourselves of every shortcut, upon arrival my hair under a big floppy hat was dripping and my clothes clung damply. (*Journal.*)

A turning point in our struggle for petrol came on 18 November, 1983 when President Cooper delivered a beautiful new 5-seated Urvan Nissan diesel-powered van for our use. Long anticipated, the red tape and politics of getting it into Ghana from neighboring Togo had been monumental. With diesel (gas oil) less expensive and somewhat more plentiful, plus the bonus that the van would go more than twice as far on a gallon of fuel than did the Range Rover, we felt emancipated. Although diesel was still not available on demand, we were enabled to carry on the Lord's work more freely than ever before. In addition, passenger-carrying capacity had increased 300%, and with the extra seats removed we could carry more than four times the cargo, an important bonus since the van often doubled as a truck.

Due to lack of petrol and horses (of which we saw but one or two), man-powered, or ofttimes boy-powered, flat-bed rubber-tired wagons were universally used to haul almost anything, from car bodies and sugar cane to household goods. A dozen boys might be seen straining and inching a heavy load up a hill, then gleefully jumping on to ride as it crested and rolled freely down the other side.

Kerosene, the fuel many used in small cooking burners and in lamps for homes and shop tables after dark, was likewise in great demand but short in supply. When some was expected at the few stations where it was dispensed, the queue of cans, buckets, pans, (even rocks to hold a place in line) would serpentine around the lot. Arguments ensued if places in line were encroached upon. The waiting for everything seemed endless and most unproductive. It was a nation at standstill—waiting, waiting, so helplessly.

Finding wood for cooking purposes was also time consuming. Bushes and small trees (and some not so small) fell prey to the cutlasses. Cut and trimmed, they were tied with vines or braided palm frond's into huge bundles. Balanced on heads, the carriers looked like walking wood stacks, sometimes going for miles. Charcoal, produced by covering heaps of wood chunks with earth and then letting it slowly smolder, was a favored but more expensive fuel. Due to the scarcity of matches it was common to borrow embers with which to start a fire.

Electricity, or the lack of it, created problems, too. Low water in the reservoirs caused power outages quite regularly, sometimes lasting for days, as noted in my journal:

> Power went off early this morning, and now at 7:15 p.m. we peer at each other across the dining table, illuminated by the "romantic" flickering of a candle stuck in a tuna fish can. I must buy candles, if any can be found. I fear what is happening to my frozen food in the little freezer. I dare not open it to look. Chuckling, we prepare for bed—no lights, no water (it too was "finished"), no petrol, no stamps, no plans or materials to build the chapel, and our one candle is burning down. We may as well get a good night's sleep. But all is fine. We are well and happy, with a secure home and plenty of food. We are rich indeed with our lovely family and the gospel. Things will work out.

Another journal notation some months later showed conditions had not changed:

> Elder and Sister Nelson came late this afternoon. It is a welcome break to have our fellow missionaries visit. They are always so refreshing to our spirits. The small noisy electric generator, cranked up to have light by which to eat supper, gasped and quit halfway through. The gas was finished, so back to the remaining bit of candle reserved for company.
>
> Out on the veranda, after supper, the evening air laden with the soft scent of jasmine brought some welcome relief from the day's heat. Under "God's light," as our watchman, Kofi, refers to the moon, the shaggy fronds of tall palms flash silvery streaks as they rustle in the shadows. But even this luxury is short-lived, as with the darkness malaria-bearing mosquitoes begin their marauding.

Just as there was a famine of food to feed the body, so was there a famine of the printed word of God to feed the spirit. Scriptures, hymnals, pamphlets or any Church publications, were treasured and difficult to obtain. The few pamphlets we had were loaned on a return basis to those we were teaching.

With people joining the Church in record numbers, we felt frustrated when unable to supply new converts with a Book of Mormon. Everyone yearned to own one, along with the other standard works of the Church. How hard it was to deny them this blessing. Through errors in bills of lading or other problems, a shipment of used Bibles from Church members in America, tied up on the docks at Tema for over a year, were finally received. The mails, too, were ponderously slow and unreliable as is the case in many countries.

Listening on our short-wave radio to the British Broadcasting Company (BBC) or Voice of America (VOA) lent an eerie sensation, almost as if we were on another planet, as the squawks and crackles would fade in and out. To tune in a station was never predictable, so eventually we gave up trying.

The lack of an operable telephone system did not help the feeling of isolation. Personally conveyed messages seemed the only sure method in Ghana, so a highly cultivated "grapevine" was helpful. Even a telegram informing us of the arrival of our newest grandson, Brandon Becker, took three weeks to arrive at our door.

But let me hasten to add, lest anyone may have gained the impression that we were dissatisfied or unhappy due to the problems herein chronicled, never did we wish to be anywhere but among our most beloved brothers and sisters in Ghana, doing exactly what we were doing.

Discussions with the members many times included these conditions, and of many parallel hard times the saints in the early days of the restoration of the Church suffered and endured; of how each of us need to be tested in the furnace of affliction, perhaps in different ways. The Lord told Brigham Young, "My people must be tried in all things." (D & C 136:31) This may bring small comfort at the time, but we are promised that "after much tribulation come the blessings. Wherefore the day cometh that ye shall be crowned with much glory." (D & C 58:4)

We loved it there. We loved the people, and I would not have traded my place with anyone. It was a most satisfying and spiritual time in our lives; one for which we will ever be grateful to our Heavenly Father.

7

Welfare Projects

And remember in all things the poor and the needy, the sick and the afflicted, for he that doeth not these things, the same is not my disciple.
(D & C 52:40)

With the organization of the Church in Ghana not yet five years old, there was already a rudimentary welfare system emerging. But solving the members' desperate economic plight mandated heroic measures.

The challenges, not only lack of rain but of irrigation equipment, farming tools, machinery, seeds, and roads over which to travel, seemed insurmountable. The almost complete absence of mechanization brought reliance on the widely used mattock (a heavy short-handled hoe) and cutlasses, which limited the size of the farms. Most preparation, planting, cultivating and harvesting were done with these simple tools. This may have accounted for the seemingly postage-stamp-size of cultivated plots we observed from the air when we first flew in.

The few tractors in evidence were usually not performing their intended purposes but were busy running back and forth on the roads hauling passengers. It must have been more profitable to transport paying customers in a trailer wagon.

A commonly used method to clear the land was to slash and burn. After the rampant weeds (they will always grow) had been chopped down with cutlasses and allowed to dry, the field was burned.

Wherever the fire had cleared, and as soon as the field was cold, corn (maize) was planted random fashion, in holes dug with cutlass, mattock or a sharp stick. Under favorable conditions, corn would soon peek through the charred ground. In some instances it even survived the drought to produce an acceptable crop. With them also, hope springs eternal.

Timing of plantings was crucial in order to catch what little rains came. Such must have been the good fortune of the Cape Coast branches, as corn from their welfare farm was ready to harvest shortly after our arrival, as noted in my journal:

> Drove about seven miles to the welfare farm to help harvest their dried corn. With cutlass in hand the saints broke off the ears then cut the stalks down. Such hard working people. They never stopped until the job was done. Care was taken that no ear was lost. Their count, my tally of 3,000 unhusked cobs, made a full load in the back of the Range Rover. Taken to Kwaw's, unloaded onto a concrete garage floor, the corn would await further processing.

An interesting incident that occurred the next day as we again harvested corn was also noted:

> While loading the corn, some people walking by stopped and asked for some. Fifteen year old Brigham Johnson gave a handful of ears to a woman. Looking a bit disdainful, she spoke rather sharply to him in Fante. Quick as scat Brigham grabbed them back. Later when asked about it, he told me that she had berated him for giving her small ears instead of large ones. Such was the fate of the ungrateful—she received none. I had heard them tell her, " This is the Lord's corn." (*Journal.*)

Brigham, an honest and delightful young man, had dreams and aspirations for the future, just as any youth anywhere. A youth's dreams, even as ours, are limited only by his knowledge and experiences. He confided in me one day that he wanted to be a big farmer and would own many, many cutlasses to grow food to help many people. Being ambitious, as well as a faithful and devoted son of his Heavenly Father, he will reap many blessings and have his dreams fulfilled beyond his present limited vision. Special to us, Brigham was ever available to help me in the house or go with us wherever needed.

President Cooper desired that every branch establish a poultry project, or whatever was feasible for them. For Sunday, 15 January, 1984, at district conference, my journal noted:

> Welfare was the theme of the conference. At a morning joint session of priesthood and Relief Society leaders, President Cooper gave much timely advice on the subject. Well-organized plans were presented by the seven branch presidents on how they were preparing for their poultry projects.
>
> To the congregation a clear message was given by President Cooper: there would be no more food shipped from America, that it was now up to the members to take responsibility toward self-sustenance. The Church, where possible, may help set up projects, but they should be managed to become not only self-sustaining, but provide much food for those in need.

Untiringly, President and Sister Cooper spared no effort to help the branches set up these projects. Due to stringent regulations, the import of machinery or other equipment was limited. The Church, however, was able to send in a shipping container of materials to help set up welfare projects. Included was a small garden tiller for each branch where a project was set up. Like kids with a new toy, the members vied with each other for the privilege to operate these machines.

With pride and satisfaction, a big part of the unused back lot of the Cape Coast Chapel grounds was soon tilled and planted. Small raised planting beds were formed, which allowed superfluous water to drain away. This was a favored system of gardening. Because tropical downpours can flood in moments, that method had merit. Garden seeds, not available in shops, were obtained at the Department of Agriculture office.

The preservation of any excess food was limited to sun drying, as no home equipment for canning or bottling was available. In his attempts to discover methods, one brother experimented with preserving tomatoes by covering hot cooked tomatoes with boiling hot oil. This was not successful.

In the coastal area, where fish was generally plentiful, much of it was sun dried. Large areas of beach were commandeered where various methods were employed in the drying. Some fish, soaked in salt water in large cement-lined baskets were then spread out on seemingly acres of palm frond mats and platforms to dry; other fish were smoked on grills over large open clay stoves. Packing the dried fish in round laundry-size wicker baskets was a work of art. Precisely placed, the heads of the small five-to-eight-inch fish radiated either toward the edge or center, making a solid firm pack.

To raise fish for food President Dadson built a concrete-lined pool in his front yard, then stocked it with fish. This project was progressing satisfactorily.

Small red hot peppers, which brought zest to so many dishes, made colorful patches when spread out to dry on the hot gravel beside the roadway. Being small and light in weight, I often wondered what prevented the peppers from being whisked away as cars, few though they were, sped by.

Elder and Sister Nelson, formerly farmers, set up a model garden-size farm plot in Accra. A shack constructed for the caretaker permitted him to live on the place, which was necessary for protection against theft. A well was drilled and a hand pump installed for irrigation.

Several solar-powered food dryers also promised great benefits as food became more available. The dryers, pumps, and drilling equipment were all part of the shipment in which the tillers were received.

Thriving projects and businesses were operated by several Church families. President Kwaw's family had a coop well stocked with a large breed of chickens, ones much larger than the scrawny specimens running loose foraging on the streets and waste piles. How thankful we were for those fresh eggs as well as a tasty chicken on occasion.

Many people in Cape Coast had a few chickens which, along with the ever-present African dwarf goats (non-milk producing, raised strictly for food) ran loose to nibble stray bits of grass, weeds, dry corn husks, or anything edible.

Although it was necessary to let animals forage on the streets, it was rather unnerving. Some drivers would madly honk and bully their way along while chickens and feathers went flying. Goats, however, could not be hurried. With looks of disdain, munching all the while, slowly they would amble out of the way. How owners kept tabs on their livestock was a mystery, but presumably hens laid their eggs in familiar territory and animals instinctively returned home at night.

While some kept their goats within a compound, one neighbor did better than that. We discovered from the sound of bleating that their goat occupied an empty room in their house.

As we prepared to leave Ghana, branch presidents were also being urged to try pig farming if other projects failed. Letters received from members since our return home indicated that some were in operation.

The Lord will truly bless and help the members in their endeavors to sustain themselves. The road that must be traveled to achieve this goal is long and hard, but the rewards well worth the struggle.

8

Commitment and Leadership

Hearken unto the words of the Lord, and ask the Father in the name of Jesus for what things soever ye shall stand in need. Doubt not, but believing...and come unto the Lord with all your heart.
(Mormon 9:27)

Commitment to the principles of the restored gospel of Jesus Christ seemed to come easily for our African brothers and sisters. Paying tithing for most began at baptism, for others long before, as noted in Max's journal:

> The Moree Branch sent their monthly report and contributions (in cash) with me to Accra, as this was the safest way. I noticed on the slips of paper, (no personal envelopes) that several of the investigators we are teaching are already paying tithing, fast offerings and budget. They are reaching out for blessings.

And again from my Journal:

> Their prayers, which reflect deep humility and dependence on the Lord, are lyrical in their praise and supplication. Phrases such as, "We have perfect faith that thou art with us" and the direct invitation to "Come, be with us," bring tears to my eyes. I look up to see if that being to whom they plead with such eloquence may actually be present. They petition for their country and people, who desperately need help. They know to whom they pray, and I know their prayers ascend on high.

Home teaching was just being organized, and this calling, as all others, was taken seriously:

> This evening two fine unmarried men about 22 or 23 years of age, Joseph Dawson Amoah and Charles Buckman visited us and announced they were our home teachers. Confessing that as this was their very first visit, they sought our indulgence if they made a mistake. After having me lead in singing a hymn, a prayer was offered. Several questions were then directed to us:
>
> 1. Are you keeping a journal? They informed us it was important to leave a history. (They were pleased when we showed them our journals.)
> 2. Do you have a backyard garden to help solve the food problem?
> 3. What are your hobbies?
> 4. Relate your experiences when you joined the Church.
> 5. Is there anything the priesthood brethren can do for you?
>
> These were all asked in sincerity to become better acquainted with us. Excellent words of wisdom and advice from our branch president, Ato Dadson, were imparted, after which the "meeting" closed with another hymn and prayer.
>
> Truly impressive, it was easily the sweetest home teaching visit we have ever had. Their dedication to do as directed was heart warming. (*Journal*, 5 December, 1983.)

At another time these same young men, in our home to borrow Church books with which to teach their friends, met a man from Liberia who had come to learn about the Church. After listening to the gospel discussion, Joseph spoke boldly to the Liberian: "If you want to know which church is true, get down on your knees and pray to your Heavenly Father and he will tell you, but you must ask in faith." No directive of mine could have been more effective, and this was from one baptized barely six months previously.

This Liberian, James Ernest Taylor, received the complete missionary discussions from Brother Johnson. When Max interviewed him for baptism and advised him that as there was no organization of the Church in Liberia it might be difficult for him to live the gospel of Jesus Christ, he firmly replied that he knew the gospel was true and wanted to teach it to his family so they too might enjoy its blessings. Baptism could not be denied him and he was sent happily on his way with our blessings and with what Church literature we could supply him.

Most teenagers displayed wisdom beyond their years, conducting their lives with decorum. This perhaps is a result of their being valued and responsible members of their family and community. This maturity was reflected in a sacrament meeting talk by 17-year-old Alex Dadson, some of whose words I noted:

> It is everyone's duty to build up the kingdom of God. We don't need a church position, necessarily, to keep us active and building the kingdom. Even the smallest child, just by his attendance at Primary, learns the principles whereby he can grow and develop in the gospel and be a good example to everyone. We each have to do our share in learning and carrying forth the kingdom to all people. No one need feel unimportant or neglected, because each has the responsibility of being a good member of the true Church. (*Journal.*)

We all need to apply such wisdom in our lives. Their desire to learn and serve the Lord in the proper way is reflected in their dreams as well. When another special man, Anthony Borketey-Coffie, about 25-years old and a science teacher at Wesley Girls High School, was at our home to deliver a message, he related a dream which was still vivid in his mind:

> In my dream I was walking through a wood and finally emerged into a magnificent open grassy field. As I walked, the place became brighter and brighter, almost like rainbow rays toward which I ran. Within these rays was a personage, a man wearing an exquisitely white robe. Around him were little children whom he was embracing. I ran fast on seeing that, and with great trembling fell before him. Holding his feet as I knelt, I said to him, "My Lord and my Master, I love you. What shall I do to become like unto thee?" Looking at me with tenderness, he said: "To become like unto me you must search the scriptures and do them." I asked again, "Please tell me what I must do," and the personage repeated the same thing, "You must search the scriptures and do them." As I again insisted he tell me something, I was directed, "To become like unto me you must do the seven things that are most like me." And immediately the dream was gone.

We sensed how real and forceful to him the dream was as he promised he was going to serve the Lord with all his heart and study the scriptures to know how best he could become like him. This remarkable young man never failed, with every visit and in each letter since our return home, to bear a humble testimony.

The simple faith of the Ghanaian saints was constant food for our souls. Daniel Renner-Sackey, another "son", related a special story of faith which occurred before he was ordained an elder:

> A few days ago, after I had retired, about 10 o'clock, my mother called me to her bedroom where she was suffering with sharp pains in her stomach. She wanted to be taken to the hospital, but first she wanted to drink some water with a little salt in it. (Medicines of any kind were almost unobtainable.) I went to the kitchen to prepare this drink and desired to bless my mother that she would feel better. Knowing that I did not have the priesthood whereby I could lay my hands on her head to administer to her, I nevertheless felt I should do something. In the kitchen I prayed, and while doing so I put my finger in the salted water and asked that it would help my mother feel better. She drank the water and again said that if she didn't feel better I would have to take her to the hospital.
>
> Returning to my bed, my sleep was not disturbed all night. In the morning when asked how she felt, my mother replied that she felt well and enjoyed a good night's sleep.

Another incident, written in a letter received soon after our return home, revealed Daniel's continued faith and dependence on the Lord:

> I will share with you an incident which happened to me in Accra recently. I had a serious cough and chest pains. I was in bed when I started coughing continuously. Certainly I was inspired by thought to pray. I kneeled down and prayed, then later returned to my bed. From that period the pains and cough stopped. I could see that faith and the Spirit which prompted me to pray, healed my sickness. Isn't that marvelous? I testify that this Church is true, the teachings are true and only by faith and abiding by the commandments and laws will your requests be granted. I say these in Jesus' name. Amen.

Their letters all contain firm testimonies of their love and faith in the Lord. How gratifying to know that their thoughts and actions are never far from the Savior.

Another such young man, Alex Asare Duodo, about 20-years old, helped clean my house each week, as did Daniel and others at times. When they were offered money for well-rendered services their reply was, "Oh no, we cannot accept money. This is the Lord's work." This revealed what truly selfless children of our Heavenly Father they are, willing to help where needed without thought of remuneration even though they desperately needed it. They exemplified perfectly the words of King Benjamin when he said, "that when ye are in the service of your fellow beings ye are only in the service of your God." (Mosiah 2:17)

Through persuasion, however, they accepted some items of food which were not available in the shops at any price. Another 20-year-old man, when given some of this food which to me was ordinary, actually danced a jig, clapped his hands and exclaimed, "Oh I am the happiest man on earth today." My heart was certainly touched.

Nearly every life has a testing in the fiery crucible of having temptations to resist and decisions to make. In Ghana it is ofttimes against age-old traditions and tribal customs. One such example was Alex who at one time did not come to my home for about two weeks. Upon his return I told him I'd missed him and had wondered where he had been. He then related this story of steadfast courage and conviction:

> Alex had gone to visit his family in their village some distance away in the bush. "And Sister Folsom, I want to tell you about the experience I had. While there, an important ceremony, with all the villagers gathered around, honored me as a special returning guest. I was to help with a significant part of the ritual, to take the bottle of libation (liquor), make a toast, partake of the liquor, then pass it around." (Picture him, surrounded by the villagers, a Latter-day Saint youth with a bottle of liquor in his hand, being expected to partake of it.)
>
> Boldly he proclaimed, "No, I cannot drink this. I am a Mormon. I belong to The Church of Jesus Christ of Latter-day Saints and we don't believe in drinking liquor." When the people insisted that he must carry out this ritual he reiterated, "No, I

> am a Mormon of The Church of Jesus Christ of Latter-day Saints and I don't drink."
>
> When the chief threatened, "We'll kill you if you don't," Alex calmly replied, "Go ahead and kill me. I'm not going to take liquor into my body. I want to keep my body clean and pure. You can kill me, but if you do, I will return to my Heavenly Father clean and pure."
>
> Whether a real or imagined threat, Alex was defying rigid tribal traditions and customs. Happily, tradition was waived. He passed the libation around but did not partake. He had firmly set his mind to do right in everything that he knew, or would die trying. Realizing his absolute dedication, tears flowed from my eyes when he said, "Sister Folsom, I was prepared to die. They could never make me drink."
>
> What a marvelous young man. We all need to be as firmly committed to our Savior and his teachings. Alex's commitment brought to mind the account of the Lamanites after their conversion, "And thus we see that, when these Lamanites were brought to believe and to know the truth, they were firm, and would suffer even unto death rather than commit sin." (Alma 24:19)

While such practices are gradually being done away with or softened, some church members expressed concern about the strictness of some tribal customs. To be ostracized from the tribe, or to receive some other penalty for non-adherence to customs, is a harsh dictum and creates difficult choices for some members.

This incident did not complete Alex's experiences while in his village. Almost apologetically he continued, "You remember, Sister Folsom, the food you gave me for helping you?" Assuring him I did, he continued, "Well, I hope you won't mind my saving it and taking it to my brothers and sisters when I went to my village. They need it a lot more than I do, and they had never seen American food."

My heart cried for him, for well I knew how he himself lived on the edge of starvation. But he had unselfishly shared with his family whom he considered even less fortunate.

Concern for others was constantly displayed. After Alex had helped me in the house another day, we were having a snack as usual before he left. Thick slices of homemade bread were generously spread with peanut butter and honey, which he was slowly eating with great relish. (They always ate slowly, as though to savor every morsel.) He asked if I had a piece of paper. To my query of what kind and how much, he replied, "Just a small piece as I want to take a taste of this delicious peanut butter and honey to my boss, as he has never tasted it." He reported later that the peanut butter sandwich he had taken to his boss was enjoyed to the fullest. How we take for granted these simple and often-scorned foods.

This valiant young man, apprenticed to Ghana Water Works, earned a mere 20 cedis a day, which would buy only two eggs or not even a half loaf of bread. He lived in a single car garage, with dirt floor, bare of furnishings, but he was rich in all the things that count most. His cheerful disposition and unflagging testimony of the gospel brought joy to all he met. What a wonderful missionary he would make, and I frequently told him so. He yearned to share his testimony as an official representative of Jesus Christ.

His opportunity came a few months after we returned home. Simply, without guile or boasting, in a letter he wrote of this blessing bestowed upon him:

> You can imagine how I am feeling at this moment, Father and Mother. It's my duty to inform you that I have now become that wonderful missionary you talked of, and we at this moment are converting people just like that. But we do all these things by the help of our Heavenly Father and also by the power and authority of the holy Melchizedek Priesthood that we bear. Isn't that wonderful? There are so many blessings to being a missionary, for instance, you cannot tell someone to be honest and faithful while you are not. I want to remain truthful and obedient all my lifetime, so that I may be found spotless at that last day.

The Ghanaian members' commitment to sacrament meeting attendance was exemplary. In Moree, with a membership of about 70, attendance on 2nd of October, 1983, was 89. Again, on October 9th, at a special sacrament meeting when babies were blessed, attendance was 120. In Sofokrom on December 4th, I counted over 70 present with a membership of less than that; again in Cape Coast First Branch on February 12th, it was proudly announced that 100% were in attendance. And so it went in all the branches. Such commitment challenges emulation.

> They eagerly reach out for the truth, wanting to obey every commandment and fulfill their stewardship in the manner in which the Lord would have them do it. Delighted to be shown correct methods, they would be implemented without delay. Such remarkably humble and teachable people. Their attitude reminds me of Proverbs 9:9, "Give instruction to a wise man, and he will be yet wiser: teach a just man, and he will increase in learning." (*Journal*.)

At the December 3rd, 1983, Cape Coast District conference with Elder Derek A. Cuthbert in attendance, we were all thrilled and proud when he announced that the 50 new Elders just sustained was a near record for the Church, being topped only by Japan when at one time 70 elders were sustained. (In a letter to us dated 26 January, 1988, Elder Cuthbert stated: "Regarding ordinations of elders, I still quote that great day in Cape Coast, but it is happening in many places now. A week ago I organized a new stake in La Paz, Bolivia and we ordained 68 new elders that day! The Lord's work is moving ahead in a marvelous way.")

How we enjoyed Elder and Sister Cuthbert as guests in our home. In December, along with President and Sister Cooper and Elder and Sister Nelson, it was indeed a special occasion as they helped usher in a spiritual Christmas season.

Again in May 1984 Elder and Sister Cuthbert were our guests along with the Coopers and Nelsons. Elder Cuthbert was pleased with the progress of the chapel in its third month of construction, and happy too that we had moved into a more pleasant and secure home. That the servants of the Lord radiate a special aura there is no doubt. They were delightfully easy to please and their graciousness and special blend of humor kept us so at ease. They had so filled our home and hearts with their sweet spirits that when farewells came it was with a touch of sadness. In that far-off land, company from "home" was always a cherished blessing. They will always hold a special spot in our hearts.

President and Sister Cooper and the Nelsons are likewise special as they never failed to lift our spirits with their love and concern. President Cooper had the ability to make me believe I was the world's best cook, even when I served the simplest of foods. Bless him! Always gentle and soft spoken, the words of a former president of the Church, Joseph F. Smith apply to this great man: "When a man lives with God his voice shall be as sweet as the murmur of the brook and the rustle of corn."

> It would be hard for most people who have never personally experienced it to comprehend the level of spirituality here among the members, and the eager seeking ones who as yet have not joined. I marvel continually at their strength of testimony and willingness to be totally committed. It is indeed thrilling. Always seeking knowledge, they love to discuss the gospel; plying us with questions and eliciting explanations of some parable, passage of scripture, or point of doctrine. Twelve-and fourteen-year olds bring us written questions, seeking answers so they can teach their friends. They are close to the Lord at all times. (Excerpt from a letter to our children.)

With such attitudes, we know they will rise to heights and be those shining beacon lights so needed in the world today.

9

Our Life in Ghana

"He who eats and drinks of Africa will never be the same."
(Anonymous)

Our first home on "Third Ridge" in Cape Coast was on an elevation higher than most of the city, but a little lower than the Franciscan Monastery perched nearby on another hill. A two-story concrete block house with three bedrooms and two baths, the house had eleven-foot-high ceilings (for coolness) which were too lofty for me to sweep cobwebs from even with my long-handled broom. Many wide glass-louvered windows, always open, provided air circulation. As in most homes of this construction, floors were of polished terrazzo. A few reed mats softened the effect, especially by beds where knees, frequently bent, were grateful for the padding. Lighting in each room came from a single 40 watt bulb hanging from a short cord in the center of the high ceiling.

The scarcity of fuel for the propane stove mandated its thrifty use. Later, the acquisition of a small electric range provided an alternative. Even so, as electricity was off frequently, we found ourselves eating cold food on many occasions in order to save precious propane to boil our drinking water. Actually, in a tropical climate, foods without refrigeration are not cold; so we enjoyed Spam, pork and beans, and many things, as they came from the can. Our two small refrigerators were a blessing when power was available.

Water supply, too, was erratic. Living on a hill compounded the problem. We often had to kneel or crouch in the tub (we weren't to sit) to shower with a hand-held sprayer, as the added height of standing reduced water pressure to zero. This was especially true in the upstairs bathroom. At times water would quit altogether, so after each use, if water were still available, the tub was filled to provide water to flush toilets or for washbowl baths.

Generally, my laundry methods were the same as the Ghanaians', or as my great grandmother's (who may have had the added advantage of a washboard). A clothesline was strung in the upstairs hallway. On days when water flowed the color of root beer, laundering and water boiling were postponed, if such a condition didn't persist too long. On our infrequent trips to Accra we enjoyed doing our laundry at the mission home in an automatic washer.

As a result of water being off at times, faucets might be inadvertently left open, with interesting consequences. One night, while dreaming I was resting on cool grass beside a babbling brook that splashed over the rocks, I awoke with a start to find that our water, having been off when we went to bed, had come on full force during the night and was spraying onto the floor like a fountain as it hit some object in the kitchen sink. Quite a pool had collected. Mopping up floors would not have been my usual choice of wee-hours-of-the-morning activities.

On another occasion, when the Coopers and Nelsons were our guests, water having been off for days, we arrived home after several hours' absence to find water flowing copiously from under the front door and off the porch. This time a bathroom faucet had been left open. Water damage to the house, built of concrete block with terrazzo floors, was minimal.

Just as the water supply was capricious, so was electricity, which also brought its "light" moments. Awakening one night to the melodic strains of "Love At Home" with full orchestral accompaniment floating through the midnight air, my first thought was, "How did our neighbors acquire some Mormon music?" Soon the source became apparent. The tape recorder in the living room had been on when the power went off earlier.

Another incident came also on a dark night. The electric substation which served the entire city had gone up in towering flames when struck by fierce lightning, completely destroying the main transformer. As a result we had been without electricity for nearly three weeks:

> Awakening during a very dark night, the hymn "Lead Kindly Light" kept running through my mind. The more I thought about

> the words and how they applied to our present circumstances, the more humorous it all seemed:
>
> Lead, kindly Light,
> Amid th'encircling gloom;
> Lead thou me on!
> The night is dark,
> And I am far from home;
> Lead thou me on!
> Keep thou my feet;
> I do not ask to see
> The distant scene—
> One step enough for me.
> (Hymns, p. 97)
>
> Nudging Max awake, I sang these words to him. We began to laugh and became almost hysterical as we thought about our situation here in the "dark" continent. (*Journal.*)

These bits of humor were refreshing oases for our spirits.

The petrol situation continued to deteriorate, with no recourse but to stay home, except for near assignments to which we could walk. However, we kept busy as we studied, prepared materials for the training of district missionaries, and taught those who came to the house. And we learned patience!

Patience! Ah yes.

Dean Packham, our thoughtful son-in-law, reading between the lines of our letters, sent us an insightful and splendid article, "Patience." It was filled with verities that we must practice:

> Patience helps us to use, rather than protest these seeming flat periods of life, becoming filled with quiet wonder over the past and with anticipation for that which may lie ahead, instead of demeaning the particular flatness through which we may be passing at the time. (Neal A. Maxwell, Ensign, Oct., 1980, p. 28.)

Without compound wall or enclosure around our home (a feature common to many), we had two watchmen, one for daytime, the other for nighttime security. However, they both proved unreliable and our home was burglarized on several occasions. Regarding this, my journal noted:

> It isn't the fact that we've had so many things stolen that bothers me as much as not knowing who you can trust or what ruse will be used next. Also my mind becomes clouded thinking about the mundane when spiritual matters should have priority.
>
> Having just completed reading "Jesus The Christ" by James E. Talmage, I want to retain the sweet feelings of love and gratitude I have for my Savior, and to continue to know him better as I strive to follow the examples of love and forgiveness that he displayed while suffering the cruelest of indignities. Studying about him has made me a better person.

As the thievery continued unabated, however, it became necessary to involve the police. The culprit, our day watchman, was found with many of our missing items in his possession. Arrested, brought into court and tried, he was found guilty and given the maximum sentence.

At the trial the magistrate berated the thief with a harsh lecture for his maltreatment of visitors in their land. Later, out in the corridor, the magistrate and lawyers, both for and against the defendant, shook our hands and apologized for one of their countryman's misdeeds, and begged that we not hold it against their country. Their kindness and concern toward us was gratifying.

While not condoning the acts, I somehow could not find it in my heart to censure the thieves too severely, but was grieved by the conditions that might prompt such actions. Actual survival was perhaps at the root of many thefts.

The lease for our home stipulated that the owner would build a protective wall around it, but after more than two years he had not done so. Living on a hill "heightened" our water problems and with lack of security we felt compelled to move. Aided by Church members, a more desirable home was found into which we moved on 18 February, 1984, again with their help. This home, in Pedu Estates, provided greater security and nicer accommodations for us as well as our guests.

A high concrete wall, with closely spaced glass shards projecting from the top, enclosed the compound to help deter unsolicited drop-ins. A concrete pad surrounded the house, with a small lawn on one side and space for a garden at the rear, which our watchman used to grow food. He planted cassava, red peppers, banana trees, and sugar cane, among other things. A large iron gate, normally kept locked, allowed us to park our van inside the compound, with space also for President Cooper or others to park when visiting.

Three ceiling fans, one each in living, dining, and master bedroom, added comfort when power was on. However, the bedroom fan, improperly balanced, swayed and protested so loudly we had some doubt as to how long it would remain in place. Large glass-louvered windows, undraped for maximum air circulation (and perhaps because drapes were not available) were protected by a grillwork of sturdy steel bars built into the concrete block walls.

Supposedly following the British system, the 230 volt electrical wiring in the home seemed unique. Plugs were round, square or triangular, and came in various sizes. They might have 3 prongs or 2, and might be either square, flat or round. Once a plug was matched to an outlet you were content to leave it there.

Now with our new security man, Kofi, a retired military man, on duty 24 hours a day, we felt more comfortable and secure. He was given time off to shop for food or visit his family when I was home. A reed mat spread on our front porch served as his bed. His reassuring words, "Madam, anyone entering your house will have to step over me, and that will not happen," provided this feeling of security.

No alarm clock was necessary, as the refreshing sound of splashing water within the compound signaled the dawn. Kofi took real pride as he washed the van shining clean and brushed it out in preparation for each day's use. Likewise, he swept and washed the compound daily, water permitting. As Kofi mowed the lawn, it was almost like the performance of a graceful ballet; on nimble feet, he swung the razor-sharp cutlass in rhythmic strokes barely above the grass roots.

To find a completely honest and trustworthy guard was difficult. We were told that the only dependable ones were retired military people. We soon found this to be true in our case. Meager though it might be, all such retirees receive a pension which they treasure highly; the slightest infraction of the law would put it in jeopardy. Not wishing to lose this pension put them on their best behavior. Many young men vied for these positions but there was no such hold on them to insure their integrity. In fact, as we found to our dismay, instead of "security guards" they simply were "watchmen," often doing a good job of watching everything disappear (even helping).

We loved and trusted Kofi as the good and faithful servant he was. There was one thing about him, however, to which we were averse. After several months of strict decorum, he arrived home one evening later than usual, after having had the afternoon off, acting rather strangely.

Walking boldly onto the porch and speaking through the open living room louvers, as is customary with callers, he startled us with "I'm home Madam, I'm home. The Lord loves you, Madam. I'm home!" repeating it with some vigor. This not being his usually reserved manner, we soon realized he was intoxicated. (As I mainly dealt with him, giving him instructions, paying his wages and other things, he usually addressed me.)

Calming him as best we could, we were first dismayed, then amused, and finally touched, as the effects of the drink wore off. Having been a military man, he reverted back to that training. Around the florescent-lit compound he marched, briskly presenting arms with his cutlass, marching in place and saluting, as befitting a disciplined soldier, all quite silently.

After not hearing footsteps for some time and wondering what he might be doing, we peeked out onto the front compound from the window of our bedroom, where we had retired. There on a chair, positioned under our window in the brightest light, he was reading the Book of Mormon which we had given him.

The next morning we accepted his apologies, along with his promise not to repeat such actions, after we told him it was not our pleasure, nor for his best good, to conduct himself in that manner.

That promise was faithfully kept until about two weeks before we left Ghana, when he again partook too freely of pito wine while on a visit to his sick mother. This could have ended tragically. At his mother's home he fell, hitting his head on the concrete floor, sustaining a skull fracture.

When found the next day, Max had him hospitalized, where he remained in serious condition, not even recognizing us as we sadly bade him farewell upon our departure from Ghana. However, sometime after our return home we were delighted to learn of his complete recovery.

As was common for most households, an open fire in the back yard, with three rocks arranged to hold a pot served Kofi's cooking needs.

For pots he valued the gallon cans in which some of our foods from the U.S. were packed. In fact, empty cans of all sizes which we washed and set out on the back porch were used by Kofi or taken home by Brigham and others. Small cans are used for cups or measuring utensils.

That the envelopes you buy in Ghana have no glue on the flap is not an oversight. Having brought a supply from home, I found they had conspired with the humidity to seal themselves up tight long before necessary.

After leaving the house one morning, the following incident occurred:

> Looking to see the time, I was annoyed to discover that I'd left my watch at home. But immediately into my mind, clearly and distinctly, came the words, "If you had worn your watch this morning, you would have lost it." I realized this could be true, as a loose clasp had been troubling me. Valued though the watch was, as to replace it here may have been difficult, the greatest value and comfort that this manifested to me was that the Spirit is ready to prompt in any kind of need we may have, whether it be spiritual or temporal. To the Lord all things are spiritual. (*Journal.*)

I still have the watch and treasure it above its monetary value.

In this land of perpetual summer, many plants and animals seen in the United States only under hot-house conditions or in zoos, abound. Among the rampant but gracefully-draped branches of crimson-flowered bougainvillaea, hibiscus, frangipani and other unusual plants and bushes lurked deadly cobras and scorpions.

Happily, the cobra and I never met, but the Nelsons in Accra were not so fortunate. Two slithered into their compound during our tenure in Africa.

And prior to our move into our second home, the neighbor there had shot the largest cobra ever seen in the area. This created considerable excitement, even attracting the attention of the news and television media. This kept us from venturing off the beaten track where such might be lurking.

However, I met scorpions. A tan three-inch fellow, swept from behind my desk while cleaning one day, his tail whipping and curling, was summarily dispatched. And another one I met when one stormy evening the welcome torrential rain had beat on my kitchen door and created quite a water puddle as it splashed under and around the loose-fitting door. After the storm abated, I took my almost worn out but treasured and irreplaceable long-handled broom in one hand, held the screen door open with the other, and swept the water out. While doing so, I was horrified as an eight-inch-long black creature came hunching and lumbering into the dimly-lit doorway, seeking refuge from the storm. From great lobster-like mandibles to curled tail, all systems were in action. With a startled shriek and one bold swish of the broom, this frightful creature, later identified as a black scorpion, went flying into the darkness.

Many times since I have reflected, how even as the scorpion, unclean thoughts, unwanted and unbidden, perhaps in dark, stormy and unguarded moments, creep into our minds. If not immediately swept out with haste and repugnance, they may find lodging and cause pain and suffering later.

Brightly hued lizards, a foot or more long, were also startling. With orange heads bobbing and iridescent blue tails twitching, they adorned our white compound wall while sunning themselves. Smaller cream-colored ones, not so colorful but also startling, crawled over the ceilings of our bedrooms on their suction-padded feet. Knowing that they helped rid the house of centipedes and other insects, although disconcerting, was nevertheless comforting, since insect spray was almost impossible to obtain. When President Cooper obtained a hand pump sprayer for us, it revived childhood memories of "Fly Tox." Yes, it still works!

Monitor lizards were another story and thankfully not as plentiful. The only one we encountered, four feet long or more, emerged from the grass and crossed the road in front of our car. A size to be reckoned with!

Wildlife in this urban area was not common, with none of the typically African animals such as lions, elephants or giraffes in the area. Smaller ones—grasscutters, tiny deer, and others, were diminishing in numbers because they were trapped for food.

In Cape Coast we saw few white people or "brunies" as we are known to the Ghanaians; in villages none at all. In many cases we may have been the first whites some had seen. One young man from Colorado served in the Peace Corps; a few women, all Europeans, taught in different schools; four Franciscan Friars were Americans. A delightful Hungarian woman, Dr. Tetteh, treated me on occasion for malaria.

Apparently hungry for conversation, Dr. Tetteh confessed to keeping me longer than usual on my visits. She would accept no pay for the first call, and only small remuneration, when pressed, for subsequent visits. The envelopes in which she dispensed medicine to her patients graphically depicted, for the illiterate, the dosage and frequency, as shown:

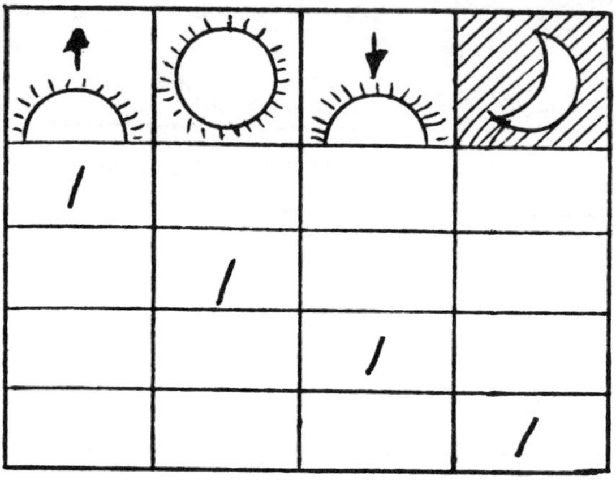

One other white, Nassib Abboud, a Lebanese, became our trusted friend and benefactor. A building contractor in Ghana for 20 years, he was adept at obtaining scarce materials in an impoverished land. With his expertise some products and services seemed to become almost magically available. Without this help our assignment would have been much more difficult. He also kept us supplied with delicious Lebanese pita bread and entertained us at many delightful Lebanese dinners prepared by his Ghanaian cook.

Because we saw so few, whites eventually looked strange even to us. We found ourselves exclaiming, "Oh look, there's a brunie!" So to empathize with the Ghanaians was not difficult. When I viewed my own face in the mirror after seeing black faces all day, I was shocked with the whiteness of it, although by now it was quite tanned. How we loved those beautiful black faces!

Children loved to rub and feel my hair as it was of a different texture from theirs. Wherever we went they flocked around, reaching out to shake hands or touch us; some would then inspect their hands to see if our white color had rubbed off. A few children, however, frightened of our strange color, would, with worried looks, hide behind their mothers' skirts. Some even cried.

As we drove along or met them, small children sang a special chant or greeting, "Hello brunie. How are you? I am fine. Thank you. Goodbye!" It was charming, though perhaps memorized without even knowing its meaning. Invariably they chanted it with never a break for reply between sentences, nor did one at any time seem expected.

Their desire to watch us became rather disconcerting at times. Sitting at the dining table in our first home without a compound wall, we would glance up while eating to see children's faces pressed close to the window, serious eyes following every morsel into our mouths. They were without guile, but curious and perhaps hungry too. They would scamper away when observed.

Red clay termite hills, 10-to 20-feet high, active and growing, dotted the countryside. Sugarloaf-like in shape, some had a tree or bush growing out of the top. Ingenious air-conditioned homes, they were built of cemented particles of earth, strong enough to bear a man's weight. termites and other wood-eating insects, which are rampant, account for most houses being built of concrete blocks or mud. Wooden homes, especially those built with soft woods, would soon be devoured.

One one occasion while walking when our petrol supply was gone, we noticed what looked like a dark ribbon an inch-and-a-half across, winding across the path and over a roadway. Closer inspection revealed a solid column of army or soldier ants marching in tight formation; millions of them on a mission I cared not to disturb or pursue.

> These ants live almost entirely by hunting, eating the flesh of any animal they can overpower as they march in broad-fronted columns on concerted raids. They do not hunt as single individuals. They destroy almost all insect life in their way and occasionally kill a larger animal which because of injury or some other restraint cannot escape. (*Encyclopedia Americana*)

Cocoa at one time was Ghana's major export crop, but through a series of misfortunes production was drastically curtailed. The country is now trying to restore production. We saw groves of these interesting cocoa trees on our trips inland. Cocoa pods, pointed and fluted, about six-inches long and looking much like Danish squash, grow on short stems right out of the trunk. Maturing in about six months, they are harvested year round. When ripe the different varieties may be orange, red or variegated green.

We watched workers split the woody pods with cutlasses to reveal 30 to 40 tightly packed beans covered with a rather sticky lemony mucous. These are actually tasty and refreshing when held in the mouth,

Cocoa trees.

but the beans themselves are bitter when chewed and require processing to make the fine cocoa and chocolate we all love.

In this inland area we also saw hundreds of acres of oil palm tree plantations, with mostly young trees but others already producing. This should be an excellent economic boost to the country.

Wonderfully efficient hand-held brooms are obtained by stripping the tough and flexible spines from the individual spikes or leaves of the oil palm tree. A good handful of these is tied together at the thick end with a small rope or strip of cloth. Not being able to buy a conventional broom, I learned to appreciate this fine tool. Adept in their use, my Ghanaian helpers could make the dust fly.

As is said, bamboo has the strength of bones and the grace of grass. The rampant growth of this plant provides variously sized poles with unending uses. Split in half lengthwise, the larger ones (4 to 6 inches in diameter) make effective roof tiles, rain gutters and fencing. Lashed together, bamboo poles for the framework for homes and other buildings. Roofs thatched with grass and palm fronds over a bamboo network are cool and, when laid properly, waterproof. Bamboo lattice walls, covered with clay inside and out, make a sturdy, durable home after being cement plastered and painted.

Coconut palms, with their delicious fruit and drink as well as fronds, are likewise versatile and ever useful. When woven, the fronds provide sturdy fences, walls for small buildings, bowers, hats, fans and hundreds of other items. Coconut shells are ready-made bowls and cups. The juice and fruit of immature coconuts seemed to be preferred, as the juice has a more delicate flavor and the soft, gelatinous fruit can be eaten by scooping it out with the back of the thumb.

Sugar cane, always available, provided a tasty and refreshing snack. Purchased at roadside tables, a stalk 16-inches long by 2-inches in diameter would refresh us while traveling the 60 miles from Takoradi to Cape Coast after a busy hot day. To wrest the sweet inner core from its tough casing was an art. My system of peeling and eating was not as efficient as those raised with the process. They could easily strip off the tough outer fibers with their strong teeth, then bite off a chunk of the core. I, on the other hand, laboriously used a knife, kept in the car for this and other purposes.

Sugar cane, albeit refreshing and satisfying, was a messy snack, because along with the outer fibers, after chewing the sweetness from the core the remainder had to be expelled, creating unattractive litter at bus stops and other gathering places.

In season we enjoyed fruit from a mango tree, which resembled a spreading oak, growing in our front yard. The tasty fruit, smaller than those in American markets, had tough skins and stringy flesh that clung to a large furry pit. From the Ghanaians we learned the most practical method to enjoy them. After squeezing the fruit until soft, one end was perforated and the contents sucked out. Rather ungracious but oh, so sweet. It brought to mind a book I had read many years ago wherein a dignified English lady withdrew after dinner to the privacy of her room, to enjoy squeezing and sucking an orange.

Our own papaya (popo) trees also provided delicious and nutritious treats. Our watchman would shinny up the fairly smooth 25-foot trunk to pick the fruit which develop and ripen first at the bottom of a large cluster tightly packed around the trunk among the huge leaves. It was not uncommon for some fruit to weigh several pounds.

Banana trees spring up almost any place, along pathways, in front or back yards and mingled with jungle trees. One began growing just outside our front fence. The fruit was small due to the drought, but the supply always seemed plentiful. Plantain, looking like bananas, required cooking to make its starchy content palatable. Oranges, although seedy and green skinned, were sweet. A large variety of pale yellow yams were plentiful, but lacked flavor.

We also enjoyed the wonderfully sweet pineapple when in season. After stopping the car at a roadside stand where they were displayed, usually at Mankesim, we would be immediately surrounded by women with pineapple-laden trays on their heads, clamoring for attention. Upon leaving, the car was always well loaded with luscious fruit selected from several different trays.

Silk-cotton trees (kapok) are beautiful as well as fascinating. Literal giants, they tower above the other jungle growth, making their presence well known. They are deciduous, but strangely not all the trees drop their leaves at the same time of the year. This characteristic is shared by many other varieties of trees, and many of the same species would be seen in different stages of their cycles simultaneously due perhaps to the almost constant temperature.

After the leaves and smaller branches have fallen from the silk-cotton tree, leaving it bare, magnificent saucer-sized scarlet magnolia-like blossoms appear which then change into long, hanging pods. These gradually swell and after a time burst open to appear like fuzzy brown bunnies clinging to the branches.

This brown fiber is billowed about by the breezes much like the fuzz from cottonwood trees, only in greater quantities. Soon after the fibers are dispersed, green leaves pop out to commence the cycle all over again. Kapok fiber, once in demand all over the world for stuffing cushions, mattresses and many other things, has been largely replaced in the modern world by synthetic materials. However, in the northern areas of Ghana, where it grows more abundantly, it is still a cash crop.

Roasted and shelled peanuts (ground nuts), are always available and they provide needed protein to those who could afford them. When purchased, they were wrapped in a cone of paper generally torn from a used copy book. A one pound margarine can (a standard measure for many things) of peanuts cost 45 cedis. When we were in Tonga a few years ago, we heard that their diet also lacked protein. The king there had wisely proclaimed that all should increase their peanut consumption to upgrade their health, to which we noticed good response, as people everywhere were seen shelling and munching peanuts. Peanuts, however, were less expensive in Tonga. In Ghana most diets are deficient in protein. Although peanuts are easily grown and are incorporated into many recipes, they are expensive to purchase.

One day in the town square of Moree we saw a large patch of "wrinkled marbles" spread out for drying. Our inquiry as to what they were was rewarded with delicious samples. These tiger nuts looked much like hazelnuts but resembled Brazil nuts in flavor.

The harmattan breezes, an indigenous weather condition of West Africa and which last about two months, herald the dry season:

> The harmattan, distinguished by thick hazy white skies, resembles our Oregon fog except fog is moist and never leaves a residue. Wafted off the Sahara Desert, the powdery white dust drapes its mantle like a pall over everything. Despite the use of creams, my eyes are red-rimmed, burning and swollen, my lips dry and cracked. With the heat, window louvers must be kept open to prevent stifling. As power is off much of the time, fans can't be operated, and when power is on we must conserve it. (*Journal*, 15 January, 1984.)

Our visit to Ghana's pride and joy, Akosombo Dam, a large hydroelectric plant and part of the Volta River Project, was impressive. We arrived after normal visiting hours, but when the manager heard that Max had been associated with similar projects in the U.S. he proudly gave us a personally guided tour. Max declared it to be a fine, well-run plant. With the reservoir level many feet below minimum draw-down, it was clear why a power shortage existed. Only one of six generators was operating and that had to supply all of Ghana and part of Togo. The five-year drought had brought almost everything to a standstill.

The quality of roads varied widely and was always a factor to be considered. The 100 miles of two-lane asphalt highway from Cape Coast to Accra, abundantly pocked with deep and hazardous potholes when we first arrived, showed gradual improvement over the months. Before we left most of it had been repaired and seal-coated with fresh asphalt and crushed rock.

Where stretches of road were particularly bad, holes would be filled with clay by enterprising young men, who, as you drove by, held out their hands for "dash." It was a worthy cause and one which we were only too happy to reward and encourage its continuance.

From Cape Coast in the opposite direction, along the coast toward Takoradi, part of the road was being rebuilt into a fine new highway by a contractor from Germany. When completed it will be a boon to travelers, but during construction the dry, rutted road sent up clouds of orange dust. When caught in a torrential downpour, as happened on occasion, we held our breath as the van careened crazily in the slimy clay.

Traveling inland to Assin Foso was an experience in itself, described in a letter to our children:

> The 50-mile trip to Assin Foso was over the worst roads I have ever traveled. There was no way to avoid the deep and abundant potholes regardless of which side of the road you chose. Hanging on for dear life, we crashed and bounced along, afraid any moment that a wheel might break; or your back or neck become dislocated. At top speed, two hours was the shortest time we could drive it, even though sparse traffic allowed freedom of the road. I'm afraid the heavy four-wheel-drive Range Rover took the punishment better than I.

Roads at any time were hazardous, but at night even more so, making night travel ill-advised. Large holes beside the road were left unmarked. Cars were often driven in the middle of the road without lights except for a momentary flash when we approached. Large vehicles and trucks zoomed past in complete darkness, leaving us trembling and wondering what went by. Cars would even be stopped on the highway. Pedestrians with dark clothes and skin, some leaning far out into your path to hitch a ride, added to the terror.

At 5 p.m. one evening, admittedly too late, we set out from Accra on what should have been the usual two-hour drive; instead it degenerated into a harrowing journey. About 20 miles out of Accra a large truck had jackknifed across the highway, blocking it completely. A crudely made sign directed us to a detour, which turned out to be long and unnerving, over strange, narrow, back-country roads, much of it in the dark. Had we known the distance involved we'd have returned to the mission home in Accra. Our petrol supply was calculated to be sufficient to get us to Cape Coast, but not much further.

Our anxiety increased because of the extra miles with no possibility of fuel replenishment, and the likelihood of a search of the Range Rover filled with cases of food the Church had sent, at machine gun manned check points. However, after friendly explanations and gifts of Spam for each guard, we sighed in relief as we were waved through the last check point and arrived home at 8:30 p.m. Certain the Lord had stretched our petrol supply to bring us safely home, we knelt with fervent thankfulness.

Generally, guards at the checkpoints were kind and courteous, many requesting religious tracts, a Bible, pen, or whatever we might have. "Pray for us," were some requests, to which we happily obliged, as their needs also were desperate.

So all considered, wisdom dictated daytime driving. Of course the curfew must not be forgotten. A 10 p.m.-to-dawn curfew had been imposed after the military take-over in Ghana. While we were there it was relaxed with the starting time moved to midnight. To be found on the streets during the curfew was punishable by fine or imprisonment.

It was essential to have a supply of boiled and filtered water at home and in the car at all times. The Royal Doulton water filter which could filter several gallons at a time was kept in almost constant operation. Bottles of water to brush teeth were kept in the bathrooms and a two-liter stainless-steel thermos jug of water was carried in our van.

Depending on our petrol supply, a visit to one or more of the district branches was on our usual Sunday itinerary. In villages where cholera was known to be present, when possible and for our safety, the sacrament cups were filled from our thermos.

Malaria and other parasitical diseases exact a heavy toll of lives in these tropical countries. Introduced into the body by an infected female anopheles mosquito, malaria is characterized by chills, fevers, nausea, diarrhea, and extreme body aches. Other parasites enter the body through contaminated food, water, the body orifices, or other means.

Although taken faithfully to ward off malaria, our weekly Daraprim pills were not successful in doing so. The second line of defense was to take three large pink Fansidar pills at the first sign of malaria. But even these were not always effective, so I fell prey to malaria seven times during our eleven-months' sojourn. But never mind, that was

Deseret Hospital.

one way to lose weight, so I arrived home a "95 pound weakling." But being a small person, that weight brought no complaints from me.

Dr. Emmanuel Kissi, a counselor in the Africa West Mission presidency, and owner-operator of "Deseret Hospital" in Accra, had been supplied with ordinarily unobtainable medicines through the aid of "Friends of West Africa," a non-profit charitable organization composed mainly of returned West African missionaries. But due to lack of petrol or being too sick when needed, we were not always able to travel to Accra to avail ourselves of his generous services. Twice, however, the colossal shots of Chloroquin that Dr. Kissi administered when we were at his hospital, although they turned my legs to rubber and blurred my vision for hours, did bring relief.

Malaria is insidious, as it catches one off guard. I was feeling fine one day, sitting in the van while it was being loaded with concrete blocks. But when my head began splitting, my legs and back aching, I knew that malaria had struck again. Other times, I would suddenly be freezing, with my teeth literally chattering in the tropical heat.

> 24 October, 1983. I should note the struggle I am having with myself. I feel so depressed, dizzy, vomiting, with diarrhea, and

> so weak I can scarcely walk across the floor. While trying to make entries in a missionary ledger I found my hands so shaky and butterflies flapping so nervously in my stomach that I began to cry uncontrollably. But then immediately I knew I had to pull myself together. Others had and are going through worse, much worse. I think of my beloved Savior and the agonies he suffered without a murmur; and of the Prophet Joseph Smith who although continually persecuted, harassed, and finally martyred, never flinched or gave up. I too must carry on. It is a great blessing to be here. This whole life must be mind over matter, or where will we be if the weaknesses of the flesh dictate and control us? (*Journal*.)

I will always be grateful to Eleanor Dadson, a registered nurse, and others of the Church for the tender loving care showered upon me during these times. Eleanor, heavy with child and uncomfortable herself, would sit by my bed, sometimes for days, and bathe my fevered brow. I was thankful too for the gentle black hands of the brethren who assisted Max in administration to bring relief to an aching body.

The Christmas season was without glitter or decorations (except for one Merry Christmas banner) and without the usual hustle and bustle of shopping, as there were few things in the markets to purchase. One discerned little change in activities as life continued on its daily struggle, except for the religious programs and celebrations which appropriately marked the blessed event. The Cape Coast branches portrayed the nativity story to reveal a more touching and deeper understanding of customs of eastern lands than we in the western world have. With President Dadson as King Herod, wearing a regal red robe, the wickedness as well as the sacredness of those times dramatically unfolded. Their acting and characterizations were superb and worthy of an "Oscar."

Responding to an invitation from the American Embassy in Accra, we attended a casual gathering of the American community in Ghana. It proved interesting and in many respects revelatory as noted in my journal:

> February 1984. Arriving at the Embassy, the Nelsons and we were surprised to find perhaps 150 American men and women from various parts of Ghana gathered on the lawn and covered

> patio enjoying snacks. American soft drinks with ice were a real treat. As we mingled and chatted, I was amazed that we felt so little closeness to our compatriots. Although many had some religious affiliation, they seemed without warmth; their conversations worldly, distant, and without substance. What a difference from our loving and spiritual black brothers and sisters!
>
> Ambassador Fritts and his wife were delightful and friendly. Speaking to the group he informed us that the U.S. government is sending $18 million worth of high protein, nutritionally rich foods—soy milk, dry milk, and many other things which cannot be obtained here but will not replace the foods they eat now or will possibly grow. Distributed through Catholic Field Services and Seventh Day Adventist world organizations, it will hopefully reach the people in direst need.

In Cape Coast we again visited with Ambassador Fritts and his wife:

> May 1984. Driving up the hill to the Franciscan Monastery, where the gathering was scheduled, we followed Ambassador Fritts' big white Chevrolet. My eyes were glued to the beautiful American flags flying on each front fender. I felt like putting my hand on my heart and shouting the Pledge of Allegiance. About 15 Americans, teachers in various schools, and including four Friars, assembled at the monastery from the surrounding areas. Small bun sandwiches, cake, and soft drinks were served while a fine group of Ghanaian gospel singers entertained us. (*Journal.*)

Following a birthday party for President Kwaw at their home I noted:

> Parties here are of a more religious nature (more to our shame) than those in America. A hymn and a prayer set the tone. After socializing and snacks, a sumptuous meal was served in courses: first, a clear spicy goat meat soup; then two kinds of spiced rice with bits of pork and chicken in a hot sauce; finishing with rice flour cakes and a sweet bread for desert.
>
> Divided into four categories, the large group of women, men, youth, and finally children, were served in that order. Afterwards, a quiz game with questions about Church history and scriptures challenged the various age groups. It was all so lovely and enjoyable. (*Journal.*)

My days, with few exceptions, were spent as a constant companion to Max, whether at the building project, shopping for building supplies, at seminars or teaching converts. We enjoyed all these experiences together. It is impossible to include even a hundredth part of the wonders of which we partook in this exotic land. We felt so contented living among these gentle happy people. Through these experiences we are richer indeed, with memories that will forever sweeten our lives.

10

Food For The Soul

Blessed are they which do hunger and thirst after righteousness: for they shall be filled.
(Matthew 5:6)

Nowhere have we witnessed a greater hunger and thirst for the word of God along with a greater lack of his printed word. Without the scriptures—those written, verified words of the Lord to fortify and sustain the teachings—missionary work could not be as effective.

We felt helpless when we learned, as previously mentioned, that a crate of Bibles sent from Church members in America had been tied up on the docks for nearly a year. I asked myself, "Why do we in America have so many and others so few? There, we have more books than we can possibly read." What were we to do? How could we solve this dilemma? A letter to our children in September, 1983, set forth the problem as well as a possible solution:

> As mentioned in previous letters, there is a lack of almost anything you can name. The people, so sweet and patient, are enduring while yearning for the one thing that will lift and ennoble as nothing else will—the gospel of Jesus Christ. Thereby hangs the crux of what I am about to suggest, a plan to aid the missionary effort in Ghana.
>
> Diane in her last letter generously inquired, "Is there anything we can send you in the way of food or literature?" I'm sure you all have wondered the same.
>
> Yes, there is something very vital you perhaps can do. Literature is desperately needed. We have no copies of the Book of Mormon,

> Doctrine and Covenants, Pearl of Great Price, and very few Bibles; pamphlets are so scarce we ask them to be returned when read. People by the dozens ask for Books of Mormon and we feel distressed that we have none. How can they gain a testimony of a book they don't have? We feel so helpless. A testimony of the divine mission of Joseph Smith and of the restored gospel is obtained miraculously through the Spirit, which is the only way anyone becomes truly converted, but we must have hundreds, yes hundreds, of Books of Mormon for them to read.
>
> Now my plan: if you, or anyone in your wards and stakes who desires, would mail us just one Book of Mormon we will soon have the mails flowing with the beautiful words of God so longed for here. Even the youth, eager to read the books, want to learn what the Lord desires them to do.
>
> If this had been done at first, not having realized the dearth that promises to continue, many books could even now be arriving. Actually, many can ill afford to buy a book, being more than a day's wages. Everyone, I feel, who donates a book for this cause will merit rich blessings for having helped one of our Lord's humble children learn about him and be more like him. All would be eternally grateful to you. This way at least we can give them spiritual food. There in America, overflowing with abundance and even waste, it's hard to imagine the desperate needs here. Impact on our missionary work would be magnificent. Books would be treasured and read to spread the word like ripples in a pond, to never-ending and everlasting benefits. I shed tears as I think of their faith and devotion to the gospel without these books. So please, will you see what can be done?

Knowing that the mails were less than dependable, we were encouraged when in due time two small packages of books arrived intact. We felt then that most books would come through, as indeed they did. Our pleas and prayers were answered through the generous response of our children and many of their ward members and friends. By mid-November books began to trickle across the great expanse of miles, first in packets of one or two or three; then the momentum picked up, and in the ensuing months we were overwhelmed to receive full cartons (35 to 40 copies each) of the Book of Mormon, Doctrine and Covenants, and many other Church books. A veritable avalanche of books poured in to fill the void. It was like a refreshing and invigorating rain after a long, hot, dry spell; first a few raindrops, bringing encouragement and hope, then, gathering forces, the heavens opened to reward the thirsty with life-giving water.

The angels, literally, who heard and answered our prayers lived in Blackfoot, Boise, and Idaho Falls, Idaho; Provo and Salt Lake City, Utah; Woodland, Washington; Pinetop, Arizona; Aiea, Hawaii; also my home ward and others in Salem, Oregon. Some packages, not otherwise identified, had only messages of love and "God bless you"; others noted: "Don't write, we know you are too busy." They had all obeyed the Savior's admonition to "feed my sheep" and "I will give unto him that is athirst of the fountain of the waters of life freely." (Revelation 21:6)

We shall ever be grateful and continue to pray for blessings to be poured out upon these generous ones who were instrumental in raising the spiritual level of brothers and sisters whom they would never know. May joy be theirs. We continue to receive expressions of thankfulness from those who have benefitted by these generous gifts.

Scriptures in hands.

Books of Mormon were presented to our brothers and sisters at baptism or other times. They would handle them lovingly and reverently and proudly bring them to church. We felt rewarded by their joy of ownership.

Postmarks on the packages denoted widely divergent times in transit. While some arrived in six weeks, others took seven months, and some arrived just days prior to our departure in June after being in the mails many months. Perhaps more arrived after we left. If so, grateful thanks go to all. Such acts of love and kindness bring blessings and rewards both to the giver and receiver.

We also received a supply of books by various Church authors. Desiring that these be made available to everyone, we set up a lending library in our home. My experience as librarian in my Salem ward was brought into use.

How blessed we are for the varied and useful experiences and training received through Church callings and service. At times one may wonder how some small position can help the kingdom roll forth, but on a mission in this or any other country, every talent and ability is found useful and can be ingeniously brought into action to be gratefully accepted by those with whom you labor.

We were pleased to see books such as *Jesus the Christ, Teachings of the Prophet Joseph Smith, Gospel Principles, Articles of Faith,* and *The Miracle of Forgiveness*, checked out of the library regularly. Because of the limited supply, only one book at a time per person was loaned so more would have an opportunity.

Gratified by the probing questions which generally accompanied the return of a book, we realized their desire to learn had evoked serious study and meditation. Books about Church history were especially enjoyed and, when returned, thoughtfully commented upon. With tears in their eyes, borrowers would offer such statements as, "I don't feel so badly that I have to suffer hunger and privations, because now I know how OUR beloved pioneers had to suffer and even die for the gospel." Tears came to mine as well. They related to and claimed them as "their" pioneers. How touching!

Illiteracy was a problem in the villages in the bush, as well as among the older generations in the cities. On every occasion during our visits to the branches I encouraged them to learn to read so they could study the word of God, as well as to gain knowledge in all aspects of life, for how could we feast upon the words of Christ and follow him if we couldn't read his words of instruction? All were challenged to bring the light of the gospel into their lives through studying and learning the English language. This would raise them out of their problems and bring progress and happiness as nothing else would. There are many, even in America, who have books, can read, but do not. They are no better off than those who cannot read.

None of our modern Church scriptures have as yet been translated and published in Fante. However, Sister Priscilla Sampson-Davis, an early baptized member and a teacher at Wesley Girls High School in Cape Coast, had translated many of the hymns into Fante and was in the process of translating the Book of Mormon. She is the mother of one of the first two full-time missionaries called from West Africa. When we left Ghana we brought with us all that she had translated and delivered it to the translation department of the Church in Salt Lake City, Utah. When completed this will be a great blessing to these dear people.

We marveled at the richness and harmony of the Ghanaian saints as they sang in perfect key, without any accompaniment. We observed but one piano, at Cape Coast University, and it hopelessly out of tune. All loved to sing, even the children, without inhibition.

There seemed to be a universal system in the branches for starting a hymn. The person conducting the meeting would ask a woman from the congregation to sing the first phrase, then he would say, "two" as a signal for all to start singing. Sometimes instead of two, "four" might be said, or "go." I never learned the significance, if any, of these numbers.

With this in mind I ventured to offer my services in teaching a music directing course. Loving music but not being a music person, neither playing the piano nor reading music too fluently, I had nevertheless for many years enjoyed being a Sunday School Music Director. Tucked away in my collection of fond memories is attendance at a music directing course taught by J. Spencer Cornwall, a former Mormon Tabernacle Choir Director.

Several sisters and some brothers accepted the offer to learn music directing. As we progressed through the basics of note value, timing, and patterns, they became excited when they were able to begin a hymn and beat a proper pattern all the way through. My humble efforts seemed to meet the approval of all and it was a thrill to see these new directors proudly conduct the hymns. They were always pleased to develop new talents and improve their ability to worship more effectively.

The Cape Coast branches had a well-trained combined choir, coached during the week by the choir director of a protestant church. Almost in awe, I observed how he taught our hymns by the do-re-me method. Every note (do-re-me) written on a blackboard was sung in that manner. Only when the tune was mastered were the words substituted. To me it was nothing less than incredible.

Many times in branch meetings I was asked to sing a hymn with which they were unacquainted in order to help them learn the tune. Me? Sing a solo? Sometimes I had Max sing with me. My efforts nevertheless seemed appreciated.

Relief Society social in Cape Coast.

Relief Society was flourishing in Cape Coast and other branches under the direction of capable leaders. Sister Elizabeth Kwaw, district Relief Society president, was carefully guiding the sisters, especially where literacy was a problem.

It was provident that Max had past experience with keeping Church records as on each mission it fell to his lot to help untangle them. My journal noted:

> Max has been working to get branch records in order. Due to wives usually keeping their maiden names to the exclusion of her husband's, and as each child may be given a different surname to honor a friend or favorite relative, it makes record keeping difficult. We are urging family units to use the same surname for all. With better records, baptismal interviews and filling forms for the ordinances would not be so laborious or time consuming.

Fante people who lived mainly along the coastline where the British influence was strongest adopted British names; without this influence, none of the interior tribes did so.

Generally in the past, genealogies and records in Ghana have not been written. However, oral genealogies, even as we heard the Maoris recite in New Zealand, can be recited for many generations. Someone in every tribe or extended family knows and can recite these lengthy relationships. It is hoped that they will be transcribed and preserved before they are lost. Family and tribal ties are precious and sacred to them. Never would they allow anyone not of their family to adopt one of their children.

As the members settle into the established order of the Church, the rough places will become smooth. What a magnificent teaching and training machine the Church is. As principles are assimilated and become operative in lives, grand order shines forth.

Education in Ghana is highly prized and honored. Even though in most instances it is offered under humble circumstances, all children eagerly attend school where available. Other than blackboards and crude benches and tables, no other equipment graces the rooms. Text books, though few they may be, for both grade and secondary classes, are furnished by the government and are stored by the headmaster after each day's use. Many schools being open to the air, we saw little means of storage for supplies and equipment. Paper and pencils are treasured. How they would revel in the tons of scrap paper and partially used pencils we throw away.

As part of school curriculum children are taught to memorize and recite from the Bible, creating a general familiarity with the book, but due to scarcity of Bibles it is difficult for the average person to own one.

Cape Coast has continued to be the center of learning in Ghana. In this and other ways Ghana seems to be a paradigm among the developing African nations. Their well-organized and smoothly-

Sculpture of boy with book.

operating schools follow the British system of grading and strict discipline. When necessary, a miscreant (there are few, I'm sure) is held by five boys while the teacher delivers 24 strokes with his cane, thus the term, caning.

All school children wear uniforms, which I consider to be advantageous in eliminating any class distinction. Each school has its identifying colors. Beginning with the second or third grades all children are taught English. We saw notations on the blackboards, "Speak English."

We learned that in Cape Coast there are about 75 grade schools; 24 segregated (boys or girls) live-in boarding high schools; several technical schools and one university, the University of Cape Coast. The latter, due to problems between students and government, was operating on a limited basis. Even so, with its resplendent architecture, sculptures and landscaping, albeit a bit neglected, it is regarded as a prestigious university.

Several of the high schools are also time-honored institutions. Wesley Girls High School was founded in 1835; Mfantsipim, with an enrollment of around 1,200 (and where President Ato Dadson is Assistant Headmaster) is the oldest secondary boys school in Ghana, having started in 1876. Adisadel, also for boys and with a long history, is still guided and directed by Anglican Church representatives from England.

Part of every boarding students' equipment is their own cutlery which they wash and put away after each meal. They also launder their own clothing which is colorfully draped over lawns and bushes to dry.

Schools, the only public buildings in some villages, were the main location for branch meetings. Sofokrom was no exception, but their school house was different than many. An open-air type building, it consisted of two classrooms with concrete block walls three feet high around three sides, and a doorless entrance into each room. A full-height wall, with a blackboard front and back, separated the two rooms and provided rigidity to the palm-thatched roof which was supported by posts at each corner. Perched on a steep knoll, the building overlooked the village, almost hidden by lush jungle. It was pleasant, as in meetings the velvet breezes wafted through our hair and rustled the pages of scriptures or thin little hymn books.

Speaking what few Fante phrases I'd learned seemed to delight everyone as we visited the branches. At church, when for the first time I greeted them "Mema wo akye" (good morning) they broke into gales of laughter. And upon my answering "Mo ho ye" (I am fine) when they asked me, "How are you?" they again laughed and gathered around me. Such was the case each time I spoke some of their language. Curious about this, I inquired of President Dadson the reason for such merriment. Did I have a funny accent, speak incorrect words, or what? Oh no, he assured me, they were just surprised and pleased to hear me speak their language so well. They enjoyed teaching me new phrases and of course I loved it.

> Nowhere have I felt closer to or loved a people more. These intelligent people (albeit some are illiterate), many of whom have received their education in England or America, seem more cosmopolitan than one might suspect. Truly they are some of God's chosen children. To be among them when they are accepting the gospel literally in droves, just as in the early days of the Church, is an unrivalled thrill. (*Journal.*)

Most young people dream of attending one of the top schools. Passing stiff government exams is a requisite for entrance and makes the honor worth attaining. Many of Ghana's better teachers, business and professional men and women are products of these excellent high schools. We have seen high school classes in session late at night and we know that by these long hours they have set standards of excellence that leave the students little free time. Praise must be given the early Christian missionaries for these advances in education; who centuries ago fostered and encouraged proper attitudes toward education. The British also left a rich legacy.

The World Bank estimates that 43% of the population of Ghana are Christians, 25% are literate, and 43% of the school age children are enrolled in school. Compared with Upper Volta, the neighbor on the north, where the literacy rate is around 6%, Ghana is progressive. These keen minds, with their desire to achieve, will restore social and economic stability to the proud people of Ghana.

11

Customs and Traditions

If you are as tall as, or taller than your father,
you are still not his equal.

The canoe must be paddled on both sides.
(Old Ghanaian proverbs)

Ghana is a land of ancient customs and traditions; many not varied for centuries. English, spoken with a soft British accent, is the official language and the one in which all legal commerce is conducted, but only the educated understand or speak it. However, they are fragmented further by about 50 different tribal languages. Their customs and habits as seen and interpreted through my western eyes were ever exciting and interesting.

Kwame Nkrumah, Ghana's first leader after the country's struggle for independence, declared that "The mistakes we may make will be our own mistakes, and it will be our responsibility to put them right." Upon the free rests a great burden to maintain that freedom where progress and development may flower. The struggle continues.

According to World Bank estimates, 54% of the land in Ghana under cultivation is used for growing food products, and two thirds of all food is produced by women. A family averages four hours a day to procure water and two hours to pound food; the demand on all family members is tremendous.

Children, not only through custom but of necessity, are an integral part of the family and are expected to contribute their full share of work. We were told that customarily children did the household cleaning while the women did other chores. We found them to be obedient and hard working.

We rarely saw children cry or fuss in any way. They are tenderly cared for at all times. The gentle system of wrapping baby securely on mother's back most all day, even while she works, may account for their deep sense of security and well being. With a child on her back it required but a half turn of the child within the wrap to provide it nourishment. Just like a little kitten snuggled close to its mother, all needs are conveniently met. Many young girls also carry brothers or sisters, almost as heavy as themselves, wrapped on their backs. In this manner children are cared for during the first several years of their lives. Many continue to be breast fed during these years as the child without proper nourishment may fall prey to the dread disease, kwashiorkor.

Women shopkeepers, tending their roadside tables, cared for their young children who played contentedly at their feet or under the tables. An older child becoming hungry would stand beside his seated mother and help himself to the ever-ready supply of breast milk. Their society seemed to be more of the matriarchal order, with several generations living in the same household, lovingly caring for one another.

I marveled how Primary children at Church, so neat and clean, packed closely together on backless benches, their legs swinging, too short to touch the floor, needed no reminders to sit reverently, hands folded in laps. When asked how they managed to instill inherent responsibility at such a tender age, they had no ready answer.

All children seem to have sibling rivalries. Ghana is no exception. One of our friends, while cooing and cuddling her newborn baby one day, was wet by him. After changing her dress and again sitting down her two-year-old son climbed onto her lap and immediately proceeded to wet her just as the baby had done. Giving the boy a little spat on the bottom, she told him he shouldn't do that. The next day the baby again wet his mother. Observing this, the two-year-old excitedly told her, "Hit him mama, hit him! He did it too."

Cooking facilities for most families were quite primitive. Some outdoor "stoves" were molded of clay into a three-humped enclosure upon which big cooking pots could securely rest, leaving a space for firewood to be poked in under the pot. Sometimes three stones sufficed

Roasting corn.

as a cooking place. Often, to save chopping, long poles were left protruding from the fire to be pushed in as the wood burned.

Corn being a staple crop, a hub of activity in every village centered around the all important diesel-powered corn grinder. The corn, normally harvested when mature and dry, is then shelled, but before being ground is water soaked, which produces a moist meal. It is prepared and eaten in a variety of ways. In most yards, big pots of porridge, stirred with long paddles, bubbled and popped over open fires. Cakes of many kinds are made, as are breads, muffins, puddings, kenkey, and hushpuppies. The list is endless.

Kenkey, a favorite, is prepared from a corn mixture, shaped into three-inch cubes, wrapped in banana leaves, packed in steel barrels, and allowed to ferment for two or three weeks. It was available on most shop tables or head trays.

Hushpuppies, also made from a corn mixture, were deep fried. We enjoyed them at Elizabeth Kwaw's one day as they came hot and fresh from a big pot in their backyard. To my remark, "These are delicious. I'll have to get your recipe," she replied, "Fine! This recipe came from my sister in Louisiana." We both had a good chuckle.

Mature corn on the cob, roasted over an open grill on the streets, is sold for snacks. On occasion Donna Nelson and I enjoyed this treat as we waited endless hours for our husbands to complete some business in the Ministries offices. And like the Ghanaians, we slowly savored every kernel, almost one by one, without salt or butter.

Although there are no McDonalds or Burger Kings, Ghanaians however are not without a counterpart: "Chop Shops." Vendors at tables along the streets dispensed a quick lunch. Steaming rice or cornmeal mush, scooped onto a fresh green section of a banana leaf, topped with spicy soup and bits of meat or fish as ordered, was tempting fare.

"Chop Shop" vendor.

Two such outdoor chop shops were in Takoradi near a large cabinet and furniture manufacturing plant where the door and window frames for the chapel were being built. As I stayed with the van on occasion for many hours, I was silent observer to many interesting scenes from life in Ghana.

These two "restaurant" women, in separate locations, each with a picnic-type table under the shade of a tree, served mid-day meals on plates. Since all the food and equipment, except the tables, were carried there on heads each day, the utensils were limited. They each had only two or three plates which, when emptied (and slicked clean they were), were thoroughly washed and rinsed and used over and over by the customers who lined up waiting their turn for chop. ("Small chop" is a snack or small amount of food.) Eating is generally done with fingers, and neatly too.

The necessary stops at highway checkpoints presented opportunities for vendors to dispense a variety of food. The most common, roasted corn cakes, partially wrapped in banana leaves with the top left uncovered to brown in the oven, tasted rather like fried cornmeal mush. Kenkey, bananas, oranges (even peeled ones), and bags of salt were proffered but sugar cane, juicy and refreshing, was our favorite pick-up snack while traveling.

Another enjoyable treat from a street vendor resembled "donut holes." The method of production was fascinating. From a bucket containing soft yeasty dough she would take a handful, then expertly squeeze round blobs into bubbling hot oil. They came out golden brown and delicious.

Between Cape Coast and Accra would be seen on occasion a small roadside barbecue with metal grill positioned on a few rocks whereon small animals were roasted. As we passed the roasted animals would be held up for our inspection and hopefully, purchase. They might be the vegetarian grasscutter (about the size of a cat, short legged, with a smooth pointed tail), a tiny deer, or some other available animal.

Cassava, a large tuber, and from which tapioca is derived, is another staple of their diet. Eaten mostly in the form of fu fu, it filled the tummy but provided little nutrition, being almost pure starch. It is as integral a part of the African diet as potatoes are of Idaho's.

To make fu fu, cassava is first boiled and then pounded for a considerable time in a mortar and pestle to break down the tough fibers. The mortar is a deep bowl formed from a smoothly hollowed-out piece of log, while the pestle is a sturdy limb or branch, peeled, smoothed, and rounded on the pounding end, perhaps five feet long and at least two inches in diameter. As the pounding proceeds a second person quickly flips over the mass between each stroke of the pestle. Plantain or yams may be added for nutrition and flavor. The women working together in coordinated motion painted a happy scene in my memory. The product, when sufficiently pounded, had the appearance of a shiny loaf of unbaked white bread, and was usually served with the traditional spicy hot soup (sauce).

Baking in large hemispherical clay ovens was quite a process. A wood fire was stoked within the oven to bring the thick clay walls to the required temperature. During the heating process numerous pans of bread, muffins and cakes of all kinds were prepared which, after the ashes were scraped out, were popped into the oven with long paddles.

As the oven holds heat well, several batches of baking can be done with a single firing.

At Anomabu two large roadside clay ovens produced deliciously light crusty round loaves of bread. Going past this bakery either to or from Accra we always drove slowly, hoping there would be some freshly baked bread. This pleasure was not often afforded as the supply was limited and the demand for the product so great.

Fresh bread at Anomabu bakery.

The foods of which we partook were well prepared, tasty and enjoyable; the cooks, of necessity, resourceful and innovative.

Watching fishermen skillfully throw round nets weighted on the rim into shallow water always fascinated me. Even the Church women on occasion showed they were quite adept at this. A popular place for bringing in deep-sea fishing nets was near the chapel site. Occasionally we were interested observers as long lines of men, women and children, tugging in rhythm and with sinews straining, would haul in the large nets that earlier in the day had been taken by dugout boat far out to sea. The chanting and rhythm in unison, I'm sure, made the task seem lighter.

Many times the catch was disappointing, as after a hard day's work some nets gleaned only a meager recompense, barely sufficient for supper. Other times, the nets disgorged an abundant harvest. How like life this is. As we all work together in harmony and love the burdens do seem lighter even if at times returns are small. We realized how we as "fishers of men" in that far-off land needed and depended upon the help and unity of our brothers and sisters to accomplish our assigned duties.

Before actual construction on the chapel began, during days when water from the one faucet was on, and mainly on Tuesdays when for some reason fishing was taboo, the Church lot became a popular gathering place for neighboring women to do their laundry.

On the short weedy grass in large pans filled with water, several women washed and rinsed their clothes, using chunks of golden brown homemade soap. Bending from the waist, knees straight, they worked hour after hour in the blistering sun. No washboards or method other than squeezing and rubbing were used. Some worked with babies wrapped on their backs, the babies cooing or snoozing contentedly all the while. As necessary, mother took time out to sit on a pile of clothes while she nursed her baby. Occasionally a blouse was removed to be washed, then bare breasted, the owner continued working while it dried. One woman must have "taken in" laundry, as I noticed a passerby drop off some bundles for her. As the fence progressed, the large piles of sand and gravel for the footings made excellent clothes dryers. But eventually when construction began in full swing laundry on the Church property, of necessity, was discontinued.

After writing to our children about these laundry activities on the Church grounds, we were amused to receive a letter from our son-in-law, Dean Packham. He couldn't understand why our daughter Diane had turned down his fine offer of a pile of gravel when her dryer quit.

It still remains a mystery to me how their clothes, using these primitive methods, come out so sparkling clean and white, while we with our modern machines can't seem to do better.

Although many homes were not blessed with modern facilities, as we know them (some had hard-packed dirt floors), cleanliness was of prime importance to the people. They bathed frequently, perhaps several times a day. Children were often observed outside in their yards, receiving a good scrub down. The white lather was gleefully rinsed off black bodies with refreshing water poured over their heads.

Headpans.

In the U.S. and other countries, fashion models practice walking gracefully by balancing books on their heads. Here it is second nature, as from early childhood everything is carried on heads, even a small empty bowl or a cup of water. A portable sewing machine with a bundle of sewing materials (a portable business) or a huge bundle of sugar cane—just everything, is carried on heads. Fascinated by the grace and regal bearing of these tall women, slender and lithe as willows, I often thought what prime fashion models they would make.

Most Ghanaians in this area have traditional as well as Christian names, depending on the day of the week on which they were born:

Day of the Week	Male	Female
Sunday	Kwesi	Esi
Monday	Kojo	Adjoa
Tuesday	Kobina	Abina
Wednesday	Kweku	Ekua
Thursday	Eyaw	Yaa
Friday	Kofi	Afua
Saturday	Kwame(Kwamena)	Ama

My name, therefore, (since I was born on Saturday) is Ama; while Max's, (born on Sunday), is Kwesi.

Kente cloth, with its distinctive crafting of highly intricate and varied colors and patterns, is woven in four-inch wide strips on small hand looms by men. The strips are then sewn together to make robes. This cloth, made from silk and sometimes interwoven with gold and silver threads, provides rich ceremonial robes for chiefs and other important dignitaries. Robes of cotton and other less-costly fibers are also a much-sought-after specialty. Max treasures the kente cloth robe, woven in blue and white with gold threads, presented to him at our departure. Measuring it, I was surprised to find its dimensions are seven by eleven feet, and its weight, nearly four pounds.

Ghanaian sculpture and carving has earned high praise for its use of traditional subject matter and skillful execution. Most are produced in wood. Elephants, a common subject, are carved to hold up tables, stools, lamps and bowls, to name a few uses. Carved wooden plaques depict family life and scenes from nature. The ever-present orange clay provides another pleasing medium, from which some of our treasured sculptures are made. One such is of a crouching man blowing a big curved horn. It depicts himself, President Pratt explained, as he presented it to us upon our leaving. Having received the gospel through us, he was now in return blowing it to all the world.

Small bronze figures of men, scorpions, turtles, fish or abstract designs were sculpted for use in weighing gold in the market place. As there was no need to weigh more than a few ounces of gold at a time, these intricately carved figures are not more than two or three inches tall.

The "Golden Stool" or throne of the Ashantis, made of solid gold, represents the Ashanti states, which are the largest states in Ghana. It is the symbol of their unity and the authority of their ruler and is considered sacred. Tradition is that this stool was conjured out of the heavens during the seventeenth century through the incantations of Akomfo Anokye, chief priest of the Ashanti king, Nana Osei Tutu. Other stools, replicas of the Ashanti ones, ornately carved from single pieces of hardwood, are treasured works of art.

We never saw real dolls in Ghana. The akua aba or fertility dolls (not toys) are sculptures of wood about eleven-inches tall; traditionally, girls and young women wear them tucked in the back of their wrap-around cloths as they would a real baby, to insure their unborn children will be beautiful.

Tribal scars, a fading tradition, were seen on occasion. In infancy, cheeks, chin or forehead were slashed, then ashes or dark dye rubbed in to irritate the wound, resulting in raised or dark scars.

One infallible method of identifying little girls, as clothes or hair generally are not dependable clues, was earrings. At birth, a baby girl's ears are pierced, then several strands of black thread looped through the holes, to be subsequently replaced by gold earrings. Baby girls also wear colorful strands of glass beads around their waist, wrists and just below the knees, to insure their growing up to be beautiful, which in my opinion they indeed do. In some West African tribes who hold mainly to matrilineal descent girls are highly valued.

Young girls from jungle villages are often "loaned" to city families where a mother has had a new baby or needs help with other household duties. They may stay for several years as servant or maid and are treated as part of the family, as they come from their own tribal village. They usually do not attend school or participate in social functions. It is considered a privilege to be chosen to come to the city and help a family.

With an innate penchant for rhythm and music, Africans love to sing and dance. It is said that more hymns are sung in Ghana than anywhere in christendom. Whether true or not, it does describe their national characteristics: love of music and religious fervor. Music and dancing are part of almost every phase of life, working, playing or celebrating, even at birth and death. We loved to hear the workers sing as they labored on the chapel and when they or the members traveled with us in the van. The children too, spontaneous and uninhibited, loved to sing and dance.

Although their native music is not widely known or perhaps appreciated outside Africa, the beat has become the root of American jazz and rock music. Many of their musical instruments are unique. A xylophone, made with varied lengths of bamboo, has calabash gourds below as sounding chambers; calabash with seeds inside are shaken in rhythm; guitar-like stringed instruments add their melodious sounds. A reed flute is one of the instruments that "talks" to sing praises, retell stories and history.

There are a variety of drums; the best known in West Africa are the great talking drums. These are carved from specially selected trees by special carvers, as it is taboo for a drummer to make his own. It is said that the drum head is usually an elephant's ear stretched across

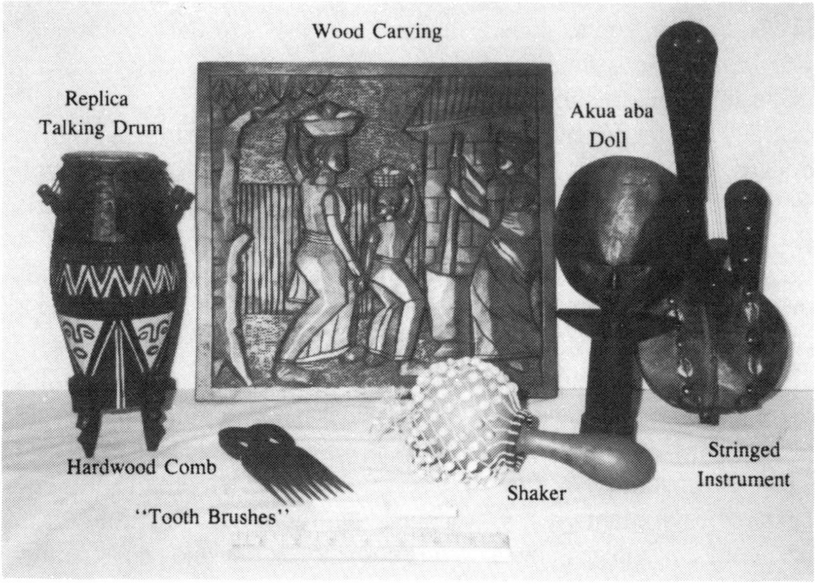

Artifacts of Ghana

Artifacts of Ghana

the rim and secured with pegs. The tightness of the pegs determine the sound of the drum. The Fante language being tonal with different levels representing words, phrases or syllables, the drums copy these accents and sounds, along with the special beat, enabling messages to be received and relayed over long distances. It is not based on a system such as Morse code as may be presumed, but on the sounds and rhythm of the spoken word.

When awakened at times during the night to the distant throbbing of drums, we wondered what drama of life or death was being announced or celebrated.

Another kind of drum, the hour-glass or squeeze drum, was named after its shape and method of playing. It has thongs stretched between the top and bottom heads. Different sounds are produced when the drum heads are tightened by squeezing the drum under the arm as it is beaten. This drum is used to accompany songs.

Church services in the protestant and native faiths are enlivened with much drum beating, clapping and marching, with people sometimes spilling out in serpentine columns into the courtyards and town squares. Any religious commemoration elicits spontaneous demonstrations.

With limited lighting in homes, shops and streets, and a strictly enforced curfew, we presumed everyone would settle down and go to their homes when darkness fell at 6:30 each evening. *Au contraire*! With the going down of the sun the city seemed to come alive. Instead of disappearing, table markets were now illuminated by kerosene lamps, many just wicks in tin cans, that flickered and glowed to pinpoint the otherwise dark streets.

People of all ages, but predominantly the young, promenaded, visited, and congregated to listen to blaring rock and roll at the few cubby-hole music stores, where a single electric bulb sliced a bright arc out of the darkness. But by curfew time the city was dark and quiet.

Older women seemed to be the only street sweepers. Using short palm leaf spine brooms and wooden dust pans, they swept up trash and deposited it in large wicker baskets. Actually, litter was minimal; no tin cans, bottles, scrap paper or such were strewn around as everything had a use. Scrap paper was used to wrap purchases of almost anything. Even corn husks from roasted corn were devoured by foraging goats. Tough sugar cane fibers, though, were spurned by even the goats.

Smooth grassless clay yards around homes were constantly being swept, and combined with erosion by wind and rain, yard levels receded so that many foundations were left so high that the steps were almost unreachable.

The deep concrete gutters for sluicing the downpours and other waste water, lining the downtown streets of Cape Coast, even in front of the old chapel, seemed hazardous. Perhaps many have suffered an ignominious, albeit temporary, disappearance when they were not wary.

Mammy wagons.

Mammy wagons, as the open air public transportation buses were called, lurched and swayed with full passenger loads, while on top, bundles piled high, barrels and even live goats clung precariously. Brightly adorned with painted slogans, the buses proudly proclaimed their owner's love for the Savior in such phrases as: "God's Time is Best," "Praise the Lord," and "Jesus the Good Shepherd." Businesses were named in like manner: "Jesus Loves Me Auto Repair Shop," etc.

Perhaps the traditional marriage customs account for much of the frustrated and hopeless feelings of many young people. Marriage is unthinkable until the man is able to provide the prescribed dowry, receive proper family approval, and supply appropriate gifts for the intended bride's family. In present economic conditions, and perhaps in all times past, men are well on in years before they are able to fulfill these requirements. Excerpts from a letter written by one of our "sons," (about 30 years of age), many months after our return home, describes their dilemma:

> Dear Daddy and Mummy,
>
> I write to brief you about the marriage proposal. I know you are keen to know about my marriage. Really, it took me a lot of time to make a choice. As you are aware for yourself, it is not easy here. It involves enough money to settle many issues. Apart from the ring and Bible, together with the dowry of about 10,000 cedis they demand 6 pieces of clothes, a trunk box, sewing machine and other articles; then some tokens to the in-laws. I have tried to get the Bible and some other articles. The only thing remaining is the ring which is very expensive, around 10,000 cedis.
>
> I will like you to send to my lady some Relief Society manuals which will help us to build a happy home, also such books which will contribute to a happy family. I want her to absorb the doctrine as she was lately baptized. She has been set apart as a teacher in Relief Society. Please Daddy and Mummy try to write and give her some advice. She is very nice in character and this will strengthen her to be a good partner.
>
> I have also adhered to your advice given and promised to strive in all my doing to live a good life. I know the Church is true and when you have faith and abide with the commandments your prayers will be answered.
>
> Your beloved son,
>
> (Signature)

Humble letters like these tugged at our heart. Without fail all letters end with a testimony of gospel truths. Is it any wonder we love them?

In the northern areas they are more strict about dowries, and as cattle are plentiful six cows is an added requirement.

When we were informed that a bride was expected to be a virgin, it confirmed our impressions, for never did we witness behavior suggestive of promiscuity or even immodesty. At times bare breasts were evident, but in this culture breasts have only their proper natural function, that of providing nourishment for babies.

Among young people smoking and drinking are taboo. We never saw a young person smoking and few adults smoke or drink. We did however observe some large calabashes filled with a foaming fermented drink being transported on women's heads. I was told that it was mostly for libations and rituals.

Funerals are also fraught with problems. In this land of deficiencies, every phase of life and death is affected. My 23 January, 1984 journal entry illustrates:

> A Church member having died, Max was asked to dedicate the grave, and as a vehicle was needed the offered use of our van was gratefully accepted. Funeral directors have no vehicles, so the family must hire a truck or cart to transport the body.
>
> At the cemetery, a shallow vault made of concrete blocks, plastered and painted white and set flush with the ground, made a proper receptacle into which, after the dedicatory service, the casket was lowered. Each relative and friend who desired sprinkled a handful of earth upon the casket. Then a concrete lid was cemented in place, sealing the vault. The dead are honored and well cared for.

Colored ceramic tile is sometimes added to the raised concrete slabs to make an ornate and protected burial site. The Fantes are known for their exorbitant and detailed funerals.

With the high mortality rate, the demand for coffins was constant. Carpenter shops making only coffins proliferated. The usual one-man operation was set up under a large tree or open bower attached to a small shack. Billows of shavings from hand planing curled around the carpenters' feet. One or two different-sized coffins were usually on display. All were broader at the shoulder area then tapered toward the feet; many were plain, others were of beautiful hardwood, while some were embellished with ornate carvings or wood inlays. One, interestingly, had a glass window on top which elicited wry conjecture as to whether it were for the convenience of the occupant or mourners.

Many ancient castles dotted the shoreline, their decaying ramparts washed by the relentless tide. Following the discovery of gold in 1471 on the "Gold Coast", the first of about 40 castles for permanent fortification in Ghana was begun soon after by the Portuguese at Elmina, a few miles west of Cape Coast. Most of the building materials, including stone for the foundation and tiles for the roof, were shipped from Portugal in a fleet of 10 vessels. It is said that Christopher Columbus commanded one ship.

Rusting cannons at Cape Coast Castle.

Cape Coast castle, also built as a fortification, has a row of rusting cannon impotently pointing seaward. Begun by the Portuguese in the 16th century, it took 118 years to build. Although now deteriorating and used as a museum, it must have been beautiful in its day, except for the dreadful fact that it was a holding place for slaves.

Cape Coast Castle.

Its stone-walled dungeons, in stygian darkness, had only one small, highly placed opening for ventilation. After my eyes adjusted to the gloom, a form became barely discernable. Into separate rooms, some 300 men and 300 women were herded to live like animals for perhaps a year before the slave galleons arrived. A long tunnel led to an opening in the castle wall near sea level where they were loaded on board ship, in what condition I could hardly bear to imagine. It was a cruel business of man's inhumanity to man. But the slave traders, seemingly without mercy, were only the middlemen; the merchandise was provided by tribes warring against each other.

The castle at Komenda, about 15 miles west of Cape Coast was, according to local residents, the refuge for Queen Elizabeth II and some of the royal family while the terrible and uncertain "Battle of Britain" raged during World War II. It would indeed have been a safe haven and a well-kept secret in this far-off peaceful land.

Ghana has suffered much but is a land of rich culture, dating back before the time of Christ. It faces a long upward climb, but a nation which tenderly and lovingly cares for its children and aged, as well as its dead, as Ghana does, has a special depth of commitment. Inherently family oriented, the gospel has great appeal as the welding power that will bind families together eternally.

12

Thanksgiving in Nigeria

Receiveth all things with thankfulness.
(D & C 78:19)

Thursday, 24 November, 1983, became a never-to-be-forgotten Thanksgiving Day.

On his previous visit to Cape Coast, President Cooper had arranged for us to go to Nigeria where Max and the architect could review the problems delaying completion of the chapel drawings.

Accordingly, on Tuesday of that week in Accra, we obtained extensions of our Nigerian visas and purchased Nigerian Airline tickets to Lagos without problems. These we considered to be no less than small miracles. But the trip, begun under such favorable circumstances, soon deteriorated.

Early arrival at Accra's Kotoka International Airport on Wednesday availed us nothing. Waiting in the pushing and jostling lines seemed interminable. For Ghanaians, waiting was a way of life, but generally they remained patient and good natured through it all. When our plane finally arrived it had but few empty seats to satisfy the milling crowd whose only desire was to get aboard. Even with confirmed tickets we were not among those privileged few.

President Cooper was to meet that flight, but we had no way of letting him know we had missed it and would try for a different flight the next day. Kwelu Ghartey, President of Cape Coast District, who was accompanying us, quickly wrote a note, gave it to a flight attendant and asked him to deliver it to a whiteman named Sylvester Cooper, who would be waiting in the Lagos airport.

Nigerian Airways had no flight the next day, but British Caledonian, flying to London, had a stopover in Lagos. In our attempts to have our tickets changed to that flight, the airport ticket agent informed us that we must go back to the Nigerian Airways office in the city to have it done. Returning the nearly 10 miles to the mission home by taxi, we then hurried to the downtown Nigerian Airways office in our van for their approval. There we were told that the airport should have first confirmed the flight, and also that British Caledonian did not ordinarily pick up passengers for the short flight between Accra and Lagos, but only overseas flights.

We drove back to the airport, only to learn that Nigerian Airways should have confirmed first. However, British Caledonian gave us an O.K. to change the flight. With time running out, paperwork seemed interminable. Rushing back to Nigerian Airways downtown office, we arrived just after the office had been locked for the day. Hammering on the door brought an agent who, providentially, was willing to change our tickets.

The following day, Thursday, after the usual gateway jostling and body search in a closed booth, we sank into our seats in the jumbo jet with a sigh of relief.

Although having enjoyed a good breakfast in the mission home, the continental breakfast, served soon after takeoff, was eaten. President Ghartey didn't eat his but later wished he had.

In Lagos, about an hour later, everyone began grabbing our luggage to "help" us through customs. We could feel a difference in temperament as scowls and tempers erupted. The message sent to President Cooper the previous day did not get through; no one was there to meet us. With only a mailing address, President Ghartey, having been to the mission home previously, assured us he could direct a taxi driver to the place. We knew the mission home had a phone and we presumed it could be used here in Nigeria. My journal picks up the narrative:

> Well! After several hours' intensive combing of the area in a taxi the mission home had not been located. Included in this time was an hour spent researching in the main telephone office, which produced no telephone number for the mission.
>
> Another comedy of errors was enacted during the day when our driver made an illegal U-turn and was signalled to the curb by two traffic officers. Although the taxi, a small four-door sedan,

was already filled to capacity with four people, one huge officer squeezed into the rear seat behind the driver and ordered him to drive to the police station. As we drove along a fierce argument ensued, little of which we understood, but to determine that the taxi driver was defying the officer required no imagination. All this occurred in heavy, speeding, six-lane traffic. Nigeria has beautiful freeways, no petrol shortage, nor any discernible speed limit.

Getting no results verbally, the officer finally grabbed the steering wheel from behind and over the head of the driver to turn the car in the direction he desired. As the driver resisted, a struggle for control of the wheel ensued. All the while, I'm biting my fingernails to the bone and praying we come out alive. This maneuvering miraculously brought us to the right outside lane. Suddenly the officer again lunged forward, and grabbing the hand brake located between the front seats, brought the car to a screeching halt. I braced myself for a crash from behind. Thankfully none came. Instantly, the driver jumped out shouting, "I'll be back," and off he galloped down the road, leaving us quite stunned.

Meanwhile, the officer, with folded arms, stood on the curb glowering at us. Actually, it was rather amusing. You could almost read the minds of curious passersby as they craned their necks at the two brunies and a Ghanaian who must be some kind of criminals.

A half hour or so later, after sweltering in the hot car, back on foot came the taxi driver accompanied by his policeman brother, who outranked the traffic officer. With six of us now wedged into the taxi, (almost needing a shoe horn) we again set out, this time for the police station. There, after vociferous arguments and considerable arm waving, it was arbitrated in the taxi driver's favor. Again we were on our way, but where to? After five hours of all this our driver admitted he was exhausted and starving, to which we three gave a resounding "Amen." Due to go off duty, where could he take us? We directed him to find a motel where we could eat, rest, and plan our next move, in that order.

Signing in at a motel, we discovered it would be $300. (American), cash in advance. This being a bit too rich for our pocketbook, we changed our minds, but were told we couldn't; we'd registered, so must pay. With no choice but to leave, we found another taxi (our friend had quickly deserted us) and had him drive us to the airport. There, at least, we could find free benches on which to spend the night, catch the flight back the next day if all else failed, and hopefully, find something to eat. A small snack shop offered ever so tiny sliced egg sandwiches and a bottle of warm Fanta orange soda, which tasted heavenly, since we'd not had anything to drink all day in the scorching heat.

President Ghartey then had a bright idea. Showing all the taxi drivers at the airport the logo of the Church printed on an envelope, he asked if any knew where the mission home was located. Thankfully one recognized it, saying he had taken someone there just the previous day.

Returning to the same area, we found the mission home at the end of a small sheltered lane, past which we had driven many times during the day; the first taxi driver having assured us that there was nothing down there. The name of the Church on the gate never looked so beautiful! Exhausted and starving, we arrived about 6:30 p.m. just in time to sit down to a grand Thanksgiving dinner; truly a day of thanksgiving. Indeed, at this juncture a bowl of bread and milk would have been a sumptuous feast.

To be with President and Sister Cooper in the lovely mission home and to meet the other missionary couples there at the home was a joy. Elder and Sister Lund Christianson, of Heyburn, Idaho, resided in the mission home in charge of affairs there, and Elder and Sister John Baxter were preparing to leave for their home in Twin Falls, Idaho, having completed their mission. Renewing acquaintance with Bishop Keith Broadway of Birmingham, England, in Lagos on Church business, and whom we had met during our two-week sojourn in England, was a pleasant surprise.

The day wasn't quite finished although as the effects of my last bout with malaria were still lingering, I felt finished. President Cooper wanted us to confer with the architect.

Setting off in the dark generally was not wise, but this time it was expedient. The streets were a madhouse of speeding traffic, horns blaring and people screaming at each other. How different from peaceful Ghana! After driving back and forth for nearly an hour, President Cooper found it impossible, because of traffic and poorly lighted highway, to find the right road. So giving up, we decided to make another attempt in daylight. I was content to return home and sink into bed. Although secretly admitting it was the worst day we'd ever experienced, we nevertheless were so thankful for abundant blessings. (Later, even President Ghartey, a Ghanaian who should be used to such things, admitted that it was the worst day he'd ever spent.)

Friday we obtained tickets for a return flight on Saturday, which at the outset didn't appear too hopeful. Arriving at Nigerian Airways ticket office in downtown Lagos, it was jammed, inside and out, with crowds of people. A man on the inside was holding the door shut. With difficulty we threaded our way through the crowd and stood by the door, peering longingly in. It must have paid off as almost immediately it was opened and we were motioned inside. There being one vacant seat at the desk where the lone agent was writing a ticket, Max took the seat and told him we had some important church work for which we needed to be home. Ours were the next tickets he wrote, and promptly, also attaching a typed note which said we were VIP and to give us every consideration. How blessed we felt for this help. (*Journal*.)

Being on Nigerian freeways was an experience in itself. With no petrol shortage, vehicles choked the highways. Nor did there seem to be a shortage of any kind; when the masses of cars would come to a "go slow" or halt due to congestion, even when away from populated areas, suddenly as if from nowhere, entrepreneurs, hawkers and salesmen appeared alongside the car, arms loaded with goods of all description: wrist watches up to their elbows, necklaces, jackets, tablecloths, hats, candy bars, etc, urging your purchases by holding them through the car window.

Finally, a conference with the architect culminated in simplifying some of the structural details, thus reducing costs for the chapel.

Arriving home on the 26th, it was good to be back in peaceful Ghana, where smiling faces greeted us everywhere. It was our 47th wedding anniversary and we couldn't think of a better way to celebrate it;

counting ourselves rich indeed to be here engaged in the most exciting work on earth—in the service of our God!

13

Anatomy of a Chapel

Little drops of water, little grains of sand
Make the mighty ocean and the pleasant land.
(Robert Louis Stevenson)

...Jesus Christ himself being the chief corner stone; In whom all the building fitly framed together groweth unto an holy temple in the Lord... *(Ephesians 2:20-21)*

A new chapel to replace the humble meeting room where twenty long years of worship had fostered spiritual growth to many would bring to fruition the fervent prayers of the faithful, signal the progress and proclaim the acceptance of the Church in Ghana. This precipitated our desire to begin construction without delay. But ah! Americans are such an impatient lot! Accustomed to a land with ample material of all kinds everywhere available, we soon discovered that to obtain any required abundant patience. All things in due time! In Ghana, even as we had experienced in other parts of the world, life moves at a more relaxed and measured pace than in America.

Realizing that "our work was cut out for us," we nonetheless thrilled at the challenges ahead. Reliance upon the Lord's constant guidance was paramount if we were to accomplish the monumental task of constructing a chapel in an impoverished land, where many basic building materials were almost non-existent or exorbitantly priced. For these same reasons the foundations and walls of unfinished buildings, whose rusting steel bars twisted heavenward, bravely begun perhaps decades ago, were now threatened with obliteration by the encroachment of trees and vegetation of all sorts. The lack of dependable transportation, communication, and most other modern conveniences bore tragic testament that the economy was harsh indeed.

Apprised soon after our arrival that working drawings for the proposed chapel being prepared by an architect in Lagos, Nigeria, were not finalized and may not be for several months, we knew preliminaries nevertheless had to proceed. Subsurface investigation and soil tests to determine load bearing capacity were needed by the architect before footing drawings could be completed. The Chief Engineer for the Highways Department in the Cape Coast area had the expertise, equipment, and personnel available to perform such work and readily agreed to do so.

In the interim, work would begin on a compound wall, or fence, to completely enclose the building site. Using concrete blocks (sand and cement, no gravel), the two sides facing the roads would be four feet high, of decorative see-through blocks, with the remainder of solid blocks six feet high. Total length of the wall would measure about 1,000 feet. The fence was necessary for the security of stored building materials, the safety of curious children and playful goats, as well as that of the completed building.

28 July 1983. Official dedication of site awaited the return of President Cooper from Nigeria. However, before beginning any work, a few stalwart men gathered to petition the Lord for his blessing. A simple ceremony under the direction of Ato K. Dadson, president of Cape Coast First Branch and building agent, began with his brief but inspiring remarks, after which the hymn "We Thank Thee, O God, For a Prophet" was never sung with more fervor. Invocation offered by Second Branch President, Holdbrooke C. McArthur marked beginning of surveying and preliminary layout work on the long-awaited project. The first Latter-day Saint chapel in Ghana had its humble beginning.

Swinging sharp cutlasses, President Dadson, President MacArthur, President Steven A. Kwaw, Kojo Amankwah, W. E. Acquah, Robert Meyer, and Daniel Renner-Sackey, men of both physical and spiritual strength, soon cleared a swath through the tall swampy grass and sugar cane growing along the property line. This people, as those we observed in the islands of the South Pacific, were also experts in wielding these long, razor-sharp knives.

Using what seemed almost crude and primitive equipment—a small hand-held compass with sighting device and a 100' tape, surveyor Dan

Ewudzie began to lay out the seven-sided plot of slightly over two acres. An entry in Max's journal stated: "I was amazed when the traverse was completed. In spite of seemingly crude equipment, closure was excellent, the angle of the final segment being off less than one degree and the length under two feet. Remarkable! Dan is a very talented young man."

Seven concrete posts, 5' long and 4" square, were to be placed at the corners for proper demarkation of property and to establish the fence line. To our amazement the same knives that chopped the brush now dug post holes. A small hand posthole auger was also used, but they seemed more adept with knives and accomplished the work faster with them.

The inequities are puzzling. The cost for seven large heavy posts was 70 cedis, a mere 10 cedis each, the same as for one egg or one bread roll, when available. Sadly, it was food for which they paid dearly, making living a desperate game of survival.

The quality of work, along with an untiring and congenial manner, gave assurance of their capability and dedication to the project's completion. A fitting climax to the day was another hymn and prayer which included a blessing on the refreshments of deep-fried hushpuppies (purchased from a passing vendor) and cool juice of green coconuts drunk from the shells after holes were chopped in them with the same cutlasses.

Just to build the fence, we soon discovered, presented tremendous challenges. Concrete for footings, posts, and blocks would require a great deal of cement, an ingredient in critically short supply, and trucks for hauling materials were virtually unobtainable. Throughout the area literally acres of broken down trucks and machinery were rusting and deteriorating for want of spare parts. Our Range Rover provided a partial solution. As able, it hauled cement, blocks, lumber, steel bars, or whatever else was needed. The lack of petrol also made progress agonizingly slow.

6 August 1983. Ground breaking, following district conference, was special. Within easy walking distance from the University of Cape Coast, where conference was held, the event attracted most of the congregation of over 300. During the brief ceremony President Cooper delivered one of the finest dedicatory prayers I have ever heard. How thrilling to be part of the "Golden Harvest in Ghana," as shovels of

Ground-breaking by Kwelu Ghartey, Cape Coast District President. Clockwise from left: Sylvester Cooper, Dr. Kissi, Holdbrooke MacArthur, Maxwell P. Folsom, President Ghartey.

soil were turned, symbolizing the beginning of the chapel-building era in Ghana.

After serving a light lunch to our conference visitors from Accra, who hurriedly departed for home before darkness overtook them, this perfect day should not have ended as it did. With what felt like sledgehammers pounding my head and legs aching and trembling, I sought the couch, thinking it only weariness. But as the next four days drifted by in a feverish nightmare my expanding vocabulary now included the dreaded word "MALARIA."

11 August, Thursday. Max, with a temperature of 104F., seems likewise to have been bitten by a mosquito. If we had to get malaria this is as good a time as any, as we are literally trapped at home with no petrol. (Happily he was afflicted only this once.)

13 August, Saturday. After 2 weeks, we obtained 5 gallons of petrol so Brother Johnson and Max went to the building site. They made plans for the branch members to build the fence with donated labor, which should pay their 2% share of building costs.

14 August, Sunday. Surveyed skills of members and uncovered many talents—plumbers, electricians, carpenters, cement workers and masons, all willing to do whatever was needed.

17 August. No petrol. So much time wasted in its search, but finally rewarded with 10 gallons.

18 August. At granite quarry, arranged for them to make our solid blocks, using granite sand, a normally wasted by-product of their rock crushing operation. We preferred it to the normally used beach sand which, contaminated by salt, makes inferior blocks.

20 August. Lack of plans and materials brought rewards in other areas. Continuing to teach, we were able to baptize twenty-one today in the ocean at Cape Coast.

25 August. Looking ahead, we obtained while available, 50 56-lb. bags of white paint (dry type, to be mixed with water), enough to paint the fence and chapel. This is the only positive move so far, except for soil testing which is in progress at the site. President Cooper is searching for a diesel-powered van for us, as that fuel is more plentiful.

30 August. A time of testing for us as well as the soil. We have no petrol and we hear that there is no crude oil in the land. Ghana, with no crude oil of its own, has the capacity to refine imported crude, but it is not available. With only three service stations in Cape Coast authorized to sell petrol to private cars, it is difficult to fairly apportion it, even when it is available. Although confined at home, we keep busy preparing missionary training materials, visual aids, and teaching. A breakthrough will come soon. We know the Lord wants his work to progress!

1 September. Received the preliminary soil test report prepared by the Ghana Highway Department. Max found it to be as thorough and comprehensive as any he had ever seen. Compensation was refused for this many-paged, carefully typed document, which required days of testing and preparation. The engineer simply stated that they wanted to help the Lord's work. The touch of the Lord's hand is upon these humble people. But without petrol, how are we to get the report to Accra and on to President Cooper in Nigeria?

2 September. We found enough petrol to reach Accra. Sent a telex to Lagos, Nigeria, with pertinent information from the soil test report. Hopefully President Cooper will receive it; even these go astray.

4 September. Max designed a decorative block to be used in the front sections of the fence. He also located a carpenter to make two sets of forms to be used in making the blocks, which will be 12" square and 2" thick. They will be hand made by a local blockmaker.

7 September. Men from both branches began digging trenches for the wall foundations. Stripped to the waist, black faces and backs gleamed with perspiration as they worked. We are praying cement will soon be available.

14 September. Arriving at the site early, before the workers, we surveyed for more trench. Using me as rodman, my experience from our Missouri mission paid off. After much negotiation with Kwamena Walker, a local contractor, we obtained one days' use of the only known crawler tractor in the area to smooth out a mountainous pile of dirt. Besides money we supplied a barrel of gas-oil (diesel) for the tractor.

17 September. 38 men, digging untiringly, completed about 900' of trench for the fence's foundation. We still have no cement or steel, but negotiations continue. Two truck loads of gravel and six of sand were delivered to site. A chocolate cake, enjoyed by all, marked Max's birthday.

18 September. My birthday was spent with the Coopers and Nelsons, who happily arrived with two sheets of partially completed chapel drawings. It's a start, but the plans are still not complete enough for estimating materials. Patience!!

21 September. No petrol, so we hiked to President Dadson's. A truck, loaded with 10 1/2 tons of bulk cement, had arrived. After 2 1/2 hours of hard, dusty work, it was unloaded into his garage using buckets, pans, shovels, etc. But how thankful we were for it. A few short lengths of reinforcing steel also were delivered. Now all ingredients to make the concrete are on hand. We're still searching for 3/4" PVC pipe to bring water from the 3" city water line.

22 September. Being informed that petrol was available, we obtained 4 gallons (the weekly ration, if you could find it), permitting us to haul lumber for the forms.

29 September. We had just enough petrol to collect the first 100 blocks and store them at the site for curing.

3 October. After nearly four weeks of intensive search, cajoling, and abundant "dash," 85' of 3/4" PVC pipe, needed to run city water to a convenient standpipe on Church property was obtained.

"Dash," or tips, is a way of life. Nothing is done, bargained for, or attempted, without "dashing" all who help—even remotely. All hands are out to receive. And shops present another inconvenience, for they are likely to be closed at any time, any day. Payment for services and material is cash in advance. Business through banks is difficult, making it necessary to carry large sums of money—literally a briefcase full of currency—as the largest denomination is a 20 cedi bill (20 cents U.S., more or less, depending on how or where you exchange your money). Hence, it became my duty to "ride shotgun," as in stagecoach days, (without gun of course) in order to protect the cargo, while Max shopped or was out of the car for any other reason.

Regarding the PVC water line extension by city water department employees, Max recorded:

> A real circus! After the saddle (metal clamp) was bolted to the main PVC line, they attempted to cut a hole in it with a length of 3/4" copper pipe that had been sharpened and heated over an open fire. Only partially successful, the pipe had been pierced

enough to permit water to squirt in all directions, but not enough to make a proper connection. With aid of my pocket knife they attempted to make a proper hole. Thinking they had done so, the ferrule (stop valve) was put on the saddle and they proceeded to connect the 3/4" pipe. During this time spurting water cascaded to drench all involved. Several women working nearby were thoroughly entertained by the antics.

When the stop valve was turned on and no water came out the end of the pipe, obviously a problem existed. Thinking it was at a second valve installed about 30' from the main line, they sawed the pipe in two at that point, but it was O.K. The pipe was then cut off at the main and another attempt made to cut a proper hole, again under a geyser of water. Success this time.

Their ingenious methods are fostered by a scarcity of both tools and equipment. Sockets on the end of PVC pipe are made by heating the pipe over a small fire and then inserting another pipe into the hot end. To make a bend the pipe is filled with sand, heated over a fire, and then expertly bent to the desired shape. (Max's *Journal*.)

5 October. The water department installed a meter just inside our property line. Also, we installed a water standpipe with a locking faucet which will preclude further use for neighborhood laundry operations. Yesterday grass, gravel, and sand piles were colorfully draped with drying clothes. We searched almost every store for wheelbarrows and headpans but to no avail. What to do? A lead took us to yet another store. They had none but while there we encountered Brother Jim Nyanka. In the area on business, he providentially spotted our van and came looking for us. After being apprised of our quest, he generously stated that the youth organization for whom he worked (somewhat similar to the U.S. Job Corps) would loan us several wheelbarrows, free of charge, which we immediately collected. Truly an answer to prayer. But still no headpans. Perhaps in Accra?

7 October. The inconvenience caused by water being frequently off mandated building a water storage tank, as steel tanks were not obtainable. A concrete slab was poured upon which a tank of concrete blocks, about 4' square and the same height, was built. Plastered watertight on the inside, it held about 200 gallons. On higher ground and filled by a garden hose, water flowed by gravity from the tank to the concrete mixing area. The necessity of installing a locking lid on tank to prevent neighbors from using stored water was regrettable, but without it we would have had none for project use.

8 October, Saturday. We took time out to teach the Branch Presidents Seminar in the morning and to help baptize 40 people in the afternoon. We obtained 6 gallons of petrol. It was a glorious day of progress in the kingdom.

10 October. A group of priesthood brethren poured concrete footings for 50' of the wall. In preparation for this work, a circular pad of weak concrete (weak so it can be easily broken up and removed when the work is completed) had been poured. On this pad, concrete is mixed by hand and then taken by wheelbarrow or headpan where needed. We obtained 12 gallons of petrol today. The Lord is indeed smiling upon us.

14 October. 290' of footings for the wall now are poured, which is 33% of the total. We hauled 40 more of the 1,200 decorative blocks required for the fence. Considering the petrol problem, this will be a slow process. Our supply of 1/2" re-bars is exhausted. Where will we find more? An opportunity to purchase a used diesel-powered concrete mixer was presented and if our offer is accepted this could speed the work, other factors being favorable.

It is interesting to note that the workers never leave the project without bathing. Taking a bucket of water, they find seclusion, strip down and bathe.

15 October, Saturday. There was a big work party at the site. 43% of the footing concrete is in place, plus 3 courses of solid blocks on two 10-foot sections of the wall. Although wasteful of both time and petrol, a search obtained a few more bars of reinforcing steel.

18 October, Tuesday. More footings were poured, but we're running out of steel.

22 October, Saturday. We had no petrol, even after being queued in line for hours on several previous days. Hearing of petrol today, we headed for the station, but the tank ran dry on the way. We rounded up 10 sturdy boys, but they were unable to push the heavy Range Rover over the intervening hill to the station. Two gallons of petrol, brought in a can from the station, got us going. At the station 6 more gallons were gratefully received.

> Considering the problems encountered to date, the task of building a chapel seems Gargantuan. A week was spent just to locate a truck to transport the loose cement, after days of bargaining for the cement. To haul all the blocks for the fence and the chapel in the Range Rover is impossible. I may well finish our mission just building a wall. How can you build without plans or materials? At present I have neither.
>
> The thought occurred to me, never uttered aloud, that I may never begin the building. How long did it take Nephi to build a ship? Neither do I know how long it will take to build a chapel. But thankfully we are almost constantly involved with baptisms. To date we have baptized 123. This is where the true building is going on—building the kingdom Of God. What a joy! (Max's *Journal*.)

27 October. We went to the Ministries Office in Accra to have passports updated and to get reentry permits. It may be necessary to leave the country.

5 November. We have more petrol than ever before. The tank is full and we have two full 6-gallon jerry cans as well. We're rich! We pray the problem is easing.

8 November. We finished pouring footings for the wall—it's been almost a month since beginning—5 months since leaving home.

17 November. A good day at the site. We hired a truck from Kwamena Walker to haul a large load of blocks. We obtained enough steel to permit the work to continue, and the wall is taking shape. Fifteen concrete columns are now cast and about half of the solid blocks are in place. Interestingly, carpenters do not need nail pouches; about half a pound of nails can be skewered into their wiry hair, like into a pin cushion.

18 November. I was not with Max today, due to work I needed to do. This evening, unable to account for all the money carried in the attache case, it was decided I must be in the car at all times to guard the cash for daily purchases. Other than that, it was a red-letter day, as into our driveway President Cooper drove a beautiful new 15-passenger diesel-powered Nissan Urvan van for our use.

21 November. Following President Cooper's directive, we journeyed to Accra to get Nigerian visas extended and to purchase airline tickets to Lagos, Nigeria. Almost miraculously, both items were negotiated without the usual delays. Another God-send that would emancipate and aid us came our way in Accra—a book of ration tickets for our new van: "a full tank every day." Our purpose in going to Nigeria will be to consult with the architect and expedite completion of the chapel plans.

29 November. Work on the wall is progressing. The crew is happily preparing to make a good showing for the visit of Elder Derek A. Cuthbert. 2,900 solid blocks now are laid in the wall and 44 concrete posts have been poured.

3 December, Saturday. District conference was special, with Elder Cuthbert of the First Council of Seventy presiding. President Cooper brought more partial drawings for the chapel. Inspection of the work accomplished at the site elicited Elder Cuthbert's unqualified approval.

Considering problems encountered thus far in building, we were thankful to be reminded during our private interview with Elder Cuthbert that our obligations were, first, to teach the gospel, and second, to build the chapel. So with those priorities, incomplete building plans and continued material shortages, we settled down to first things first. Ah yes! How often we desire to work within our own timetable as, perhaps selfishly, we struggle to complete some task, without heeding what may be the Lord's will. Patience, patience!! "Bear with patience...and I will give you success." (Alma 26:27)

5 December. The first water bill was a shock! It stated we had used 9,959 cubic meters of water for a cost of 6,903 cedis. Water for our home costs about 7 cedis per month. We discovered that the meter, a new one which registered zero when installed, was running backwards. Reporting this, the unbelieving water department checked it. Sure enough, as the water ran, so did the meter—backwards. With the meter reversed and the billing re-figured, we were most happy to pay 41 cedis for water actually used.

16 December. Max is struggling to compile the materials list from incomplete drawings. Steel, wire mesh, nails, etc., must be ordered from Togo, the country bordering Ghana on the east. Building materials of all kinds are readily available in Togo and at reasonable prices. With unbelievable problems, triumph will be all the sweeter!

18 December. After waiting six months for this day, we just received final chapel plans from President Cooper. (Praises be!)

21 December. How harmoniously the men labor together. With muscles straining and heads erect they carry heavy headpans of concrete, many singing all the while. Such hard work, even with the nearly new concrete mixer, which we purchased at a bargain price. Masons have finished plastering several sections of the perimeter fence. It looks lovely.

22 December. We departed at noon for Accra to deliver the materials list to Elder Nelson who will fly to Lome, Togo, to purchase the needed items.

31 December. A close of the year progress report: The wall is looking good, with solid blocks all in place and all columns poured except the two main gate pillars. Most solid block panels have been plastered. No decorative blocks have been laid, but 800 are stored at the site, ready for use. Considerable time has been spent revising long-awaited drawings in order to eliminate unobtainable materials and to meet site, function, and climatic requirements. The changes are subject to approval by President Cooper during his January visit.

6 January. The work is halted pending receipt of materials. Delivery of 10 tons of bulk cement has been held off until a long-sought and momentarily expected shipping container in which to store it arrives.

15 January. We reviewed revised plans with President Cooper. He was pleased with the changes, especially economy measures that eliminate or simplify elaborate and costly construction methods.

17 January. Not being able to leave sooner due to political unrest, Elder and Sister Nelson flew to Lome, Togo, to order building materials. As borders between countries are closed it must be shipped by boat. The expected arrival date is around February 6th.

20 January. We've had no diesel for two weeks. In visiting with a neighbor near where we will soon be living, we learned that he, a road contractor, has a large diesel storage tank. "You come live by me, no problem. You have gas-oil." He then filled our tank and would accept no pay. Small miracles?

24 January. We purchased toilets, lavatories, and ceramic tile for the restrooms and font, all reasonably priced, at a ceramics factory between Cape Coast and Accra.

30 January. John Adams Abraham has been hired as construction foreman. The workers are willing, but due to the language barrier we needed a skilled and knowledgeable Ghanaian on the project; also construction techniques differ from those in the U.S. This will free Max from many pressures; procuring materials has become almost a full-time job.

Following several weeks of suspension due to materials shortages, work once again is under way. The site is now staked with an interesting Ghanaian control system, and construction on the chapel is being readied. Batterboards are installed completely around the work area, not just at the corners as is usually done in the U.S. Nails in the batterboards mark the location of every footing, foundation wall, and interior partition. Only 4 1/2 months of our time remains and we're just now ready to begin actual building.

Excavation of footing trenches.

1 February. Four men began digging footing trenches for the chapel.

2 February. The digging crew has been increased to six. Lumber for the construction shack was purchased at a small sawmill, whose location is hard to believe. Perched on the pinnacle of a steep hill, we wended our way toward it through a busy market place, our horn blaring to convince marketeers to pull back their pans of cornmeal, tomatoes, peppers, bananas, oranges, etc., from the center of the steep, rutted, clay roadway. How logging trucks ever manage to get up there is a mystery.

3 February. Eric Hawkson has been hired as Quantity Surveyor, a position similar to but more exacting, than that of Estimator. Everything, down to the smallest nail, is calculated and accounted for.

Carrying 50 lb. building blocks on heads.

6 February. The digging crew finished all the footing trenches—600' in length, 2' wide and 3' deep. Water has been off for four days and the tank went dry. We must build a larger one to have sufficient water for mixing greater amounts of concrete that will now be needed for the chapel.

9 February. Nassib Abboud, a Lebanese building contractor, offered his assistance in obtaining materials. This could prove helpful. Laying decorative blocks on the fence continues. Built a 2,000 gallon concrete block tank; 10' square and 3' high, it will hold a full day's supply of water. This tank will also serve as a temporary baptismal font until the permanent one in the chapel is ready.

A 14' by 14' construction shack has been completed, having an attached palm-frond-covered bower to shade the carpenters' bench. Lumber, only rough sawn at the mill, must all be hand sized and planed on the job as we have no electrical tools, nor electricity with which to run them if we did. Due to the power shortage the city is not presently connecting any new electrical services. This also leaves us without night security lights. A steel-bending bench has been set up and heavy gloves obtained for the men assigned to this task, as steel becomes blistering hot in the sun.

10 February. Pouring of the footings began with the limited supply of cement on hand. The project passed its first two city inspections: layout and excavation. Our security guard, who proved to be less than trustworthy, was replaced by a retired army sergeant, Anthony McCarthy, who will be on duty 24 hours a day. (He slept during the day while work went on and cooked his food over an open fire)

13 February. Errands galore! Ours being the only transportation, it takes time to haul blocks, lumber and incidentals, and to track down enough cement to keep going until our big shipment arrives. (We even haul around police, water department workers, and building inspectors). Max says he feels like a spinning top.

14 February. We went to Takoradi to order door and window frames.

15 February. The long-awaited load of cement arrived from Takoradi, 8 tons of it, this time in paper bags.

16 February. They're pouring the footings that do not require steel. When steel arrives the masons will begin laying chapel walls, which should quickly rise. Realizing we will not finish the building before we leave, the workers nevertheless desire to see it as nearly completed as possible and are working hard.

20 February. The ship that was to bring our steel from Togo is reported "missing." The blocks are rising on the classroom wing. In one trip we manage to haul 50 of the 50-lb. blocks or 80 smaller ones, keeping us busy. We found enough steel to carry on a little longer.

Hopefully the missing ship will soon arrive with our steel. All the foundation blocks for the chapel are laid and look wonderful.

28 February. We went to Accra to check on the steel shipment. At the dock in Tema we saw "our" ship which had been in port 10 days. Although two telexes confirmed the steel's arrival there was none aboard. The captain promised to have it on the next trip.

1 March. Except for the font and permanent underground water-storage tank, all footings are poured and the foundation walls are built up to floor level. Most "hard-core fill" is in place. A nicely lettered Church sign has been erected at the site. Decorative block laying on the fence continues, but the block-maker, who carefully makes them by hand, cannot keep up with demand. So on every hand we wait, wait, while time is getting short. We must be patient.

5 March. We arrived at the Tema dock early in the a.m. The ship is in port with our steel! Although it was dumped on the deck loose and tangled, we thrilled to see 16 tons of steel bars, mesh, wire, and nails. A beautiful mess! Perhaps tomorrow it will be ours.

8 March. After anxiously awaiting arrival of the truck with the steel, we again headed for Accra and Tema to determine the problem. The steel is still sitting on the dock where, off-loaded from the ship, it is now in an even bigger mess. Port policy does not permit loading directly from the ship to a truck. But never mind, no truck is to be had anyway.

9 March. Elder Nelson, after intense search and negotiation, procured a suitable truck. The whole operation was an ordeal, complicated by the manner in which the steel was shipped. Instead of being tied in bundles (as we paid the Shipping Agent to have done) the 3,000 bars of reinforcing steel of various diameters from 1/4" to 3/4", all 20' long, were shipped loose. By the time it was on our truck it had been handled 6 times. With each handling it became more tangled and twisted, like a bunch of spaghetti. Above very vocal objections of the truck driver, in addition to 16 tons of steel products a 20' shipping container (long awaited for needed storage) was rather unceremoniously jammed onto the rear, with nearly a third of it hanging over the end of the 40' semi-trailer.

At this point the driver stated that it was so late in the day he would wait until morning to drive the load to Cape Coast. Such a layover would incur a heavy security risk. At our insistence he headed out with the load, accompanied by a trusted Church member to assure delivery of our precious cargo. In addition, we followed the truck through Accra and part way to Cape Coast before going ahead to prepare for unloading.

By the time the truck reached Cape Coast, daylight was nearly spent. A large forklift, borrowed from a nearby soap factory, quickly unloaded the heavy container but was not able, nor did it have time, to unload the steel. With darkness approaching, the forklift, without headlights, had to travel back to the factory on a busy highway.

The 11 men rounded up to unload the truck literally wrested the steel for 4 1/2 hours. Each piece had to be separately extricated from the tangled mass in the only light available—our van headlights. It never ceased to delight us how congenially and happily the men worked together, never complaining or impatient, always helping each other as needed. At the finish all were weary, but immensely thankful that now, after two months, we had our precious steel.

We find many joys here but sometimes pressures seem to crowd in almost too heavy to bear. "In the process of life, we are not always the already-tempered and helpful hammer which is shaping and pounding another. Sometimes we are merely the anvil." (Neal A. Maxwell, "Patience")

12 March. Full steam ahead pouring concrete floors—the classroom wing first. My head ached just watching the African system. Whether mixed by hand or machine, 75 to 100 lbs. of concrete was carried on heads in large pans where needed. With open trenches and piles of dirt everywhere, wheelbarrows became impractical. One woman worker carried pan for pan with the men. The 50-lb. building blocks were also carried on their heads, sometimes two at a time.

Without lights, and now with added materials stored on the site, a second watchman was necessary for nighttime security. Consequently, a stately and devout moslem was hired. Before beginning his nightly duties, usually clad in white tunic and cap, he knelt on a prayer rug for about 15 minutes facing eastward and with forehead to mat, he paid homage to his deity.

13 March. A quick trip to Takoradi to check on the door and window frames revealed work on them has not begun. They will soon be needed.

Eric Hawkson (estimator) and John Adams Abraham (construction foreman) with Maxwell P. Folsom

14 March. Classroom floors have been poured and the walls are rising. Pouring the chapel floor is underway. President Cooper is delighted with progress he saw today. With all costs now determined we find that the 1,000 lbs of nails from Lome cost 45 cents a lb. as compared to $5.00 per lb. we had been paying locally. Other steel items showed similar price reductions.

20 March. We hauled decorative blocks in the a.m., then went to Takoradi to get the classroom window frames. They're not ready. We Checked for cement because we're running low. None found.

21 March. Max and our electrical contractor had a successful shopping trip in Accra. They returned with all the needed electrical materials, including ceiling fans. When electricity is available we will be ready.

22 March. We went to Takoradi to collect 6 of the promised window frames, but discovered they were made the wrong size.

6 April. No work was accomplished all this past week—no cement. We borrowed 50 bags from Mr. Bafloe, our contractor neighbor. Work was resumed on a limited basis. All in all, the work is progressing; but patience! "Patience is a willingness, in a sense, to watch the unfolding purposes of God with a sense of wonder and awe—rather than pacing up and down within the cell of our circumstance." (Neal A. Maxwell, "Patience")

9 April. Located 20 bags of cement in Takoradi.

10 April. Hauled the last decorative blocks. Now fence can be completed and area made more secure.

11 April. We went to Takoradi, accompanied by a sound-system technician, to look for sound equipment. We experienced no success in that area, but did return with 10 bags of cement. The building now is well defined with its ultimate shape easily visualized. The classroom walls and the font are nearing completion. Walls in the restroom and office area are about 60% complete and the plumbing is roughed in.

We're now negotiating for the terrazzo floor installation. They are artists in this craft. We're also looking at furnishings. To determine comfort and style, Max has built a simple mock-up of a pew and our foreman, John, will make a finished sample.

12 April. A further search for materials again took us to Accra. We also found components for a drinking fountain for chapel courtyard.

16 April. We took delivery of roof timbers, corrugated aluminum roofing sheets, and glass louvers for the windows.

19 April. With no delivery of cement during previous two weeks, we were dismayed to discover that none will be available for another two weeks. Our supply is exhausted and all workers except the carpenters again are laid off. With time so short it is disheartening. With a few bags we could finish the classroom walls and begin the roof. "But if we hope for that we see not, then do we with patience wait for it." (Romans 8:25)

We can now devote almost full time to teaching and baptizing, which never ceases to be exciting.

21 April. In spite of everything, excellent progress has been made. The permanent underground water storage tank, located beneath the chapel floor, is finished. It holds enough water to fill the font twice. The font is low enough so stored water can flow into it by gravity, allowing its use even when city water is not running. The permanent font, although not yet tiled, was sufficiently complete to allow its use today to baptize 10.

New font.

25 April, Wednesday. We went to Takoradi to collect window frames. None are finished. They said, "Come back next Wednesday."

4 May. We obtained 20 bags of cement after 4 days of negotiations—only enough for today's work. But more is promised.

Plastering the walls of the classrooms.

5 May, Saturday. We were excited to receive 150 bags of cement. This should help make a good showing for Elder Cuthbert and President

Cooper when they visit next Tuesday. The rostrum end of the chapel with its concrete tiers is poured. With the chapel walls now up to window-top level the room appears much larger.

8 May. Elder and Sister Cuthbert were pleased with progress made in three months of construction. It was a real joy to have them again visit.

11 May. We travelled to Takoradi to take some diesel fuel for the truck that will haul our cement. They have none and we have a little extra.

12 May. We were overjoyed to see the truck bringing 200 bags of cement. With care this may last until we go home.

15 May. Corrugated aluminum roofing is being installed on the classroom wing. A security wall, at my suggestion, is being added near the restroom entrances to prevent public access without first entering the main courtyard. Elder Cuthbert concurred in this.

Elder and Sister Folsom at pulpit.

22 May. There has been no electric power in entire area for over two weeks, which has resulted in a scarcity of water. This curtailed concrete work, but the carpentry is proceeding and plastering of the classrooms is underway. Roofing in this area is nearing completion.

24 May. We went to Takoradi for the promised and desperately needed window frames. None are completed. With time slipping away, frustrations must be quelled. However, we picked up some doors ordered long ago and two sheets of plywood to form the spire.

26 May. Our foreman completed some sample pews—very functional and beautiful.

31 May. The work is going slowly. Diesel is again in short supply, but a shipment from Nigeria finally arrived. After none for about a month, we felt blessed indeed to get our tank and two jerry cans filled.

1 June. Max and President Dadson, with a truck rented from Nassib Abboud, brought a load of tongue-and-groove hardwood boards from Takoradi. This will be used for the ceilings, wall panelling, and for the rostrum.

Our diesel worries should be over. We obtained a 300-gallon tank which will be kept in our garage. Kwamena Walker has agreed to keep it filled; if any one can do it, he can. A large ebullient gentleman, Kwamena, a tribal chief, always looked resplendent in lavish robes and gold chains. We enjoyed many pleasant dealings with him. On occasion my banana bread found his ready acceptance. He would tell Max: "Have Madam send more of her delicious bread."

8 June. Some window frames were finally obtained. The chapel walls continue to rise. Work on the restrooms and branch president's office is progressing well. The building is perhaps 2/3 complete. We went to Takoradi to pick up office chairs as promised. Only one was finished.

14 June. Our replacements, Elder and Sister Carl and Jean Halladay, from Washington, Utah, have arrived. Orienting, visiting branches, packing, and tieing up many loose ends kept us busy.

It is hard to realize our year is drawing to a close. So much has happened; so much is left to do. Our hearts rejoice for this incomparable experience and the opportunity to practice patience.

14

Joseph William Billy Johnson

Come, O thou King of Kings! We've waited long for thee,
With healing in thy wings To set thy people free.
Come, thou desire of nations, come;
Let Israel now be gathered home.
(Hymns, p. 59)

Joseph William Billy Johnson and his faithful band of adherents often sang this hymn as a plea to heaven during the many long and discouraging years of waiting for succor and recognition from Church headquarters in Salt Lake City.

Much has been written about this remarkable man, Brother Johnson, and this work would not be complete without a brief recounting of the part he played in the exciting drama of establishing The Church of Jesus Christ of Latter-day Saints in Ghana. In his own words, Brother Johnson explained:

> In the year 1964 I came into contact with a man called Dr. E.F. Mensah, who came to my home in Bubuashie, a suburb of Accra. This man had received literature of The Church of Jesus Christ of Latter-day Saints from Lillian E. Clark of England. He introduced the Church to me and gave me some of the books to read. I remember I have from him pamphlets: "What the Mormons Think of Christ," "The Testimony of the Prophet Joseph Smith," "Articles of Faith" and a copy of the "Book of Mormon."
>
> As I read the literature I was convinced that it was true, and began to receive wonderful manifestations that I was to do the

> work of the Lord. I vowed that I would do whatever I was commanded and felt compelled to teach those things I had learned.
>
> I started in a humble way, constrained by the spirit to go from house to house, from street to street and from town to town. Persecutions began. As no one had heard of the Mormons they branded us anti-Christ. But in spite of persecutions, pamphlets being written against us, turned out of meeting rooms, and being put upon in the streets, our numbers grew wonderfully. (Oral and taped interviews)

This situation was succinctly and eloquently stated perhaps a hundred years earlier when John Taylor, third president of the Church, said, "When truth shall touch the cords of your heart they will vibrate, then intelligence shall illuminate your mind, and shed its lustre in your soul."

In 1969 Brother Johnson left Accra to establish the Church in his hometown Cape Coast. Through diligent and untiring labor he organized many branches in that area. But persecutions followed him. Other churches taunted him by saying that the Salt Lake City church would never recognize them. They offered to pay handsomely for his services and for his congregations to join with them. Undaunted, he continued on.

Brother Johnson's wife, disenchanted with him and perhaps siding with the opposition, claimed he was spending too much time on a fantasy in which she did not believe and so left him and their four children. While he was praying desperately one night for comfort and guidance as to what course to follow, a man dressed in white appeared to him and asked, "Are you going to follow me or go after the woman?" He knew what he must do.

Now with the children to care for, he carried 11-month-old Brigham (named for Brigham Young) in his arms each day as he performed his missionary activities. What the Lord told Nephi applies so well to Brother Johnson: "Blessed art thou, Nephi, for those things which thou hast done; for I have beheld how thou hast with unwearyingness declared the word which I have given unto thee, unto this people." (Helaman 10:4)

As the years passed with nothing other than bits of literature and letters of encouragement from Utah, Brother Johnson and his group of believers became disheartened. Nevertheless, they carried on valiantly, gaining even more followers.

Knowing that baptism was essential, his converts clamored for that saving ordinance. Although Brother Johnson knew he was without proper authority, he finally agreed to baptize them in order to hold the group together. But knowing the ordinances were not valid, all were happily rebaptized by the proper authority after the missionaries arrived.

The "Reverend" Johnson became renowned as a man of great faith with healing powers. The sick and afflicted were brought to him to be healed. He recalled one such occasion, (also recorded earlier by John H. Cox). On 23 December, 1975, a 16-year-old student came to the Johnson home complaining of mental and physical disorders. Accompanied by her mother, they stayed in his home, where on Christmas day she died. The girl had been declared dead by a doctor about 7 p.m., apparently of a heart attack.

Brother Johnson recalls praying continuously from 4 p.m. until midnight on her behalf. He appealed to the Lord to save her life because she had come to him seeking help and he was concerned that members of his congregation and the community would doubt that the Lord was still powerful among them.

Getting up from his knees about midnight, Brother Johnson took the girl into his arms so that she was standing. A few moments later she awoke and started to praise the Lord. She also declared many unknown facts about the persons there with them, which they confirmed to be true.

Another manifestation also served to strengthen the group. Brother Johnson's brother, dead since 1961, appeared to him and said he wanted to be baptized, adding, "Dear Brother, don't give up. This is the only true church in the world and also here in the spirit world. I am being taught the gospel here and I know it is true. Don't give up!"

Many acts of healing and manifestations continued, as without ceasing the group prayed for recognition from the Church. Each time a miraculous event occurred, it had a salient influence upon the struggling devotees. Brother Johnson is convinced that the Lord provided these in order to maintain the vigor within the group.

Approximately three months before President Kimball received the revelation granting the priesthood to "all worthy males," Brother Johnson felt impressed to tell a congregation to whom he was preaching that within four months Salt Lake City would recognize the Church in Ghana and send representatives to help them.

He related his feelings when on that memorable night, 9 July, 1978, he heard electrifying news. Upon returning home from work late that night he felt an unexplained inner excitement, so, staying up, he listened to the BBC radio station. Amidst the crackles of static and fading voices, clearly the news came through that The Church of Jesus Christ of Latter-day Saints had granted the priesthood to the blacks.

Could this really be so? After 14 years of struggle and prayer he could scarcely believe his ears. Tears of joy flowed from his eyes and exultation filled his breast. His faith had been rewarded and his sacrifices all recompensed. Excitement raced through every fiber of his being; all thoughts of sleep vanished as he contemplated what great events would now unfold.

Following closely behind the revelation, representatives of the Church arrived as Brother Johnson had predicted. Ted Cannon and Merrill J. Bateman were sent to Ghana and Nigeria on a two weeks fact-finding mission. They brought back reports of the establishment of "The Church of Jesus Christ of Latter-day Saints" with its own charter and constitution legally formed according to the laws of Ghana. Hundreds of active members in several congregations were ready and waiting, desiring baptism.

Simultaneously, and each without knowledge of the other, the Lord had been similarly preparing a group in Nigeria to receive the gospel of Jesus Christ.

Two missionary couples, Elder and Sister Rendell Mabey and Elder and Sister Ted Cannon were dispatched to Ghana and Nigeria in December 1978 to bring power and authority to a joyfully awaiting multitude.

Brother Johnson, among the first of many in Ghana to be baptized, was immediately set apart as president of the Ghana West District. Branches with ordained leaders, and Relief Societies were set up and began flourishing.

Upon our arrival in Cape Coast some four-and-a-half years later, Brother Johnson, his wife (he had remarried) and children were among the first we met. Indeed we found him to be worthy of his almost legendary reputation. A man of unwavering faith, with courage born of absolute knowledge of the power of God, he continues with humble, selfless devotion to serve the Lord and his fellowmen.

Always at our side, he gave indefatigably of his time, talents and means. Life in a foreign land where cultures and conditions were different and often difficult would have been almost impossible without his guiding influence.

Our daughter Lisa sent an item from her newspaper about Ghana which mentioned Brother Johnson, and asked if we knew him. My letter answered: "Yes, we are proud to say, we know Joseph William Billy Johnson well. He is one of our dearest friends and literally our right arm. Tireless, he is with us constantly in helping interpret, teach, negotiate, etc. We just love him. He is one of the dearest, sweetest men I've ever known. Truly, a great man of God!"

An energetic and dynamic man, Brother Johnson was always on the go. Self employed as an appliance repairman, he was also struggling to build a new home and run a small farm. He was never too busy to lay aside his work and accompany us wherever necessary to do what was needed. He would give us the last gallon of petrol from his own car so that we could carry on the Lord's work. Our praise and love for him can never be overstated or diminished.

Brother Johnson was set apart as District Missionary Supervisor when the first district missionaries in Ghana were called on 6 August, 1983. In this position his missionary zeal continued to flourish as he guided many into the gospel.

He related an experience to us which carries a message for all:

> While teaching a man, Brother Johnson received the inspiration that this man would not accept the gospel. He prayed that the gentleman would be given the ability to see the truth. Two weeks later, the man told him that he'd had a dream wherein he had climbed up a very steep hill, on the top of which was the kingdom of God. He wanted to enter but the gatekeeper told him, "No, you must go back and get the proper baptism to get in. You must go back as you cannot enter the kingdom without it."
>
> Although shown what he must do, he told Brother Johnson that it would be too hard to be baptized and then climb back up that long steep hill which he thought he must do before entering the gate. Consequently, he rejected the gospel.
>
> Yes, the Lord will ever guide us if we are willing to abide by his teachings, but he does not promise the road will be easy. Just as the Savior told the rich young ruler, "...sell all that thou hast,

> and distribute unto the poor, and thou shalt have treasure in heaven: and come, follow me. And when he heard this, he was very sorrowful: for he was very rich." (Luke 18:22,23) (*Journal*.)

Homage is due this great man for his indomitable spirit and the great sacrifices he endured as he became instrumental in bringing the gospel to Ghana, and for his unflagging determination which continues to this day.

15

The Village of Moree

Wherefore, ye must press forward with a steadfastness in Christ....feasting upon the word of Christ.
(2 Ne.31:20)

In the fishing village of Moree resides a schoolmaster, Theophilus Nii Odoi Pratt. He was a delight to us from the moment we met him at our home in Cape Coast in July, 1983. At the invitation of Elder and Sister Williams, he had come to receive his first gospel lesson. Instantly impressed with his sincerity and enthusiasm for learning, we also recognized his potential leadership qualities.

On a previous Sunday, he later related, his curiosity had brought him to his school where he surreptitiously listened to church services through the glassless windows. What he heard kindled his appetite for more.

As the lessons progressed Brother Pratt excitedly absorbed the gospel. It seemed we could not teach him fast enough, as after four discussions he requested baptism. He bore a firm testimony of the truthfulness of the gospel and felt that "God has a work for me to do." We too felt this to be true.

A dynamic man of perhaps 50 years, he is rather small, slender and wiry, and typical from his way of life, had muscles of steel. Besides being an educator, he had an orange grove to care for.

On August 25th, Mr. Pratt came to the house for his last discussion before his scheduled Saturday baptism. His testimony was positive and enthusiastic. He had but to hear the truth to recognize and accept it;

the Lord had prepared him. On his baptism day, 27 August, 1983, I noted in my journal:

> To Moree for the baptism of Theophilus Pratt. The ocean there is beautiful with waves to delight a surfer, powerful and curling that break off shore. Brother Pratt fairly glowed as he came out of the waters of baptism. Confirmed, given the Aaronic Priesthood and ordained to the office of priest, he appeared to be one happy man. (P.S. As it turned out, this was the only time we baptized one person at a service. All other times we had groups. Brother Pratt did not want to wait even a few days for others who were almost ready.)

Less than one month later, September 25th, Brother Pratt became the new president of Moree Branch, which was in acute need of leadership. The former branch president had moved away sometime previously and the two counselors had each felt insecure to fill the top position. But they would now serve as counselors to President Pratt.

Regarding Moree, this special village was noted in my journal:

> Situated about seven miles east of Cape Coast, Moree was first settled by the Dutch centuries ago. Known as one of the main fishing harbors on the coast, it is a quaint, yes even ancient-looking hamlet. Its numerous but tiny clay homes cling together, as though for support, on the steep hillsides, looking like they could have existed during the time of Christ. Narrow winding streets and pathways of rutted orange clay were worn powdery smooth from the soft patter of bare feet. Everywhere were large open cylindrical fish-drying stoves made of clay or steel drums from which the permeating scent of smoking fish hung in the air.
>
> Crowds of scantily clad, curious children pressed around us, faces wreathed in smiles, but eyes kept watchful vigilance. One could almost picture the Savior among them, patting children's heads, walking among acres of drying fish nets, relating a parable to the fishermen mending their nets with needles that flash in the sun, smiling at mothers as fish drying grills were stoked and babies nursed from ample bosoms. Here everyone appeared better fed, having more protein in their diet. It was a contented scene.

Drying fish on grill.

Proud of their harbor and fishing boats, the members were eager to give us a closer look at the harbor area, accessible only on foot. Escorted up and over a precariously rutted and steep hillside (I with the aid of a most welcome arm), we then picked our way down to the water's edge. Arrayed before our eyes appeared what looked like acres of splendid fishing boats, each hewn from a single log, gently undulating in the waters of the protected cove.

Moree Harbor.

Paul Akromah-Toffah, a counselor to President Pratt, proudly pointed out his boat bearing the name "LATTER-DAY SAINTS" in bold letters; another boat carried the name "ARK OF MORMON." The Apostle Paul would have been proud of them, as he himself proclaimed: "For I am not ashamed of the gospel of Christ: for it is the power of God unto salvation to everyone that believeth." (Romans 1:16)

Church services in Moree were held in a classroom of the school where President Pratt, as headmaster, was led into his conversion through curiosity about the gospel and the "smiling white Americans."

As he related to us, Martha Mills, the Relief Society president, had repeatedly come to him to rent a room or two where Sunday services could be held. Each time he refused, because there was no way he would rent to another church. Already there was too much drumming, clapping and singing, since several other groups met in buildings surrounding the common open courtyard. He finally gave in, more to get rid of her, when she assured him there would be no drumming or clapping.

We came to understand his position, as many Sundays we also experienced the rather boisterous celebrations that took place in the courtyard and nearby buildings. Besides the ever-changing religious festivals, a kaleidoscope of activities unfolded to view through the open doors and windows of the school room "chapel." Small bleating goats and foraging chickens darted among the busy children who usually had pails of water or bundles of wood on their heads. Heard was the rustle of the stately palms whose swaying fronds seemed to brush the billowy puffs of cotton that floated in an exquisitely azure sky. Down the courtyard a fishing boat was being carved and hollowed from a single wawa log perhaps 60 feet long and six feet in diameter. It was a masterpiece of artistry. Tropical birds flashed their bright plumage as they chattered. The steady thump thump of fu fu being pounded and the ever-present lazy flies that droned in aimless circles in the room are all indelibly imprinted in my memory.

Sitting in the small schoolroom on a Sabbath day was in itself an education in ethnic culture. Invited to sit up front with the conducting officers, we occupied the only chairs with backs. Facing the congregation, who sat on benches, placed us in close proximity that enabled us to study their friendly but shy expressions. Each child was fresh and clean in his prettiest clothes. All were beautiful children of God.

Old Cape Coast chapel, interior.

Although many of the congregation were unable to read or write either in Fante or English, they lived happily and simply. The gospel is a powerful influence that brings out the best in everyone. In each village we visited, the Church members seemed to have a special bearing that accompanied their way of life.

My journal of October 9th records a special day in Moree:

> Brothers Johnson, James Ewudzie and David Imbrah came along to help with ordinance work today. As yet there are no elders in Moree. This is to be a "bless the babies" sacrament meeting, since no babies in Moree have previously been blessed.
>
> Prior arrangements with President Pratt brought a surprising attendance of 120. (Membership was slightly over 70.) The walls of the little schoolroom fairly bulged. Among the group blessed were my dear little namesakes Emma (my middle name) Folsom-Eshun, born 3 September, and Marjorie Akromah-Toffah, born a few days later on 12 September, 1983. (The fathers are both counselors to President Pratt.) It was an honor to have these precious babies carry my names. Blessed also were 25 other babies and small children, and three young men ordained to the office of priest in the Aaronic Priesthood. The closing hymn of

> this thrilling meeting, "The Spirit of God Like a Fire is Burning," swept through us all like a fire.

Many more babies and children, whose parents had not understood the meaning of the occasion, were yet to be blessed so there would be another such day, President Pratt promised.

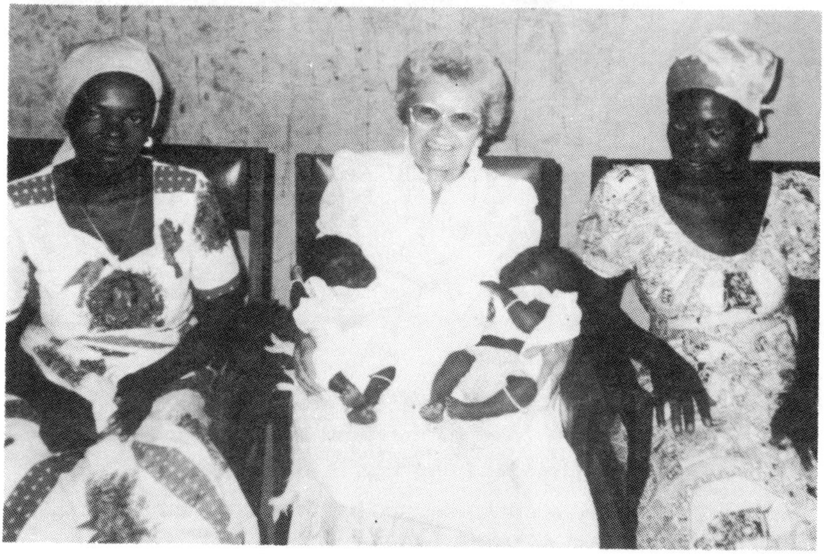

Marjorie W. Folsom with her namesakes.

Less than three months after President Pratt's baptism his wife Dorcas and their two sons, Armstrong and Gospel, entered the waters of baptism to unite a happy family in the gospel. Sister Pratt, also a school teacher, will be a great asset to the Moree Branch.

23 January was another interesting day in Moree:

> In sacrament meeting the visitors were all called to speak and bear testimonies. With Brother Johnson as interpreter, I took my text from 2 Nephi 18-20 wherein Nephi emphasizes that after baptism all is not done, but that we must "press forward, feasting upon the word of Christ." But, I queried, if we cannot read, how can we feast upon the words of Christ? As in other branches, I challenged them to learn and study, and for President Pratt to begin literacy classes.
>
> Max was to have been the next speaker, but President Pratt leaped to his feet as he took up the challenge. On the blackboard

behind him he printed: "PRESS FORWARD FEASTING ON THE WORDS OF CHRIST." Pointing to each word, he explained it, and had them repeat it many times, which all did with great enthusiasm. Then in Fante he dramatically and positively spoke for some time, driving home his message, to which they listened with serious eyes. He had given them their first English lesson right in sacrament meeting and there seemed a general stir of approval. What a great man he is!

After the meeting we accompanied Paul Akromah-Toffah to his home so Max could give a blessing to Marjorie, who was ill with "the fever," as malaria is called. Parking in the town square of bare clay, we followed Paul through a section of this primitive village with its clay huts and narrow rain-rutted steep pathways weaving in and out between the wee dwellings. Reaching his home we entered a tiny but neat living room. The four small occasional chairs with an equally small table in the center occupied the entire room except for a set of low shelves against which a chair pressed. The only other room, a bedroom, divided from the living room by a curtain, was barely the size to contain a bed. It was a lovely home with everything necessary for happiness. Most of us could certainly rearrange our priorities where "things" are concerned.

Dear little Marjorie was listless and whimpering, her large black eyes now drooped almost shut. As I cradled her in my arms she snuggled down and sighed as though she would go to sleep. Although her head felt cool, her hands were feverishly hot. As Max gave the blessing with Paul holding her, the little angel seemed to again relax and ceased the whimpering she had taken up. Her eyes opened wide and appeared as if she were gazing down the corridors of eternity, understanding every word. (*Journal.*)

When we returned to Moree on business two days later, I noted:

Parking in the city square, we sent a boy to find Paul, knowing we could not find our way through the maze of pathways. Upon greeting Paul, we asked him how Marjorie was. When he said, "Little Marjorie died yesterday," thinking I had misunderstood, I repeated the question. Oh what shock and anguish to find our little darling had indeed died yesterday at 4:30 p.m. of jaundice brought on by severe malaria. I couldn't believe it. My precious one that only two days before I had cuddled in my arms, was already buried. (Children are buried as soon as they die.) It was so sad. African children are prey to many terrible diseases. With the mortality rate so high, life expectancy in West Africa is only about 45 years.

But as her father Paul said, "We will see her again. She is with her Heavenly Father now." Yes, this is true. She has completed her short mission on earth by gaining a body, being one of the faithful souls who needed no testing in this life. Our Heavenly Father called her back to him. (*Journal.*)

My journal of Sunday, January 29th, recorded:

Packed a few sandwiches, filled the water jug and left for Moree, never knowing when we might return. Accompanying us were President Kwaw and Brother Johnson.

After the regular meetings a "Thanksgiving" service honored little Marjorie. (No funerals are held for children, just memorial services). Without prior arrangement, when asked to be the only speaker, my chosen text, Moroni Chapter 8 from the Book of Mormon seemed appropriate. Herein the prophet Mormon writes to his son Moroni, stating that all children are saved in the kingdom of God through the atoning sacrifice of our Lord Jesus Christ. To enter the kingdom of God baptism is not necessary if they are too young for accountability, as they cannot sin. Baptism is for the remission of sins. "If not so" says Mormon, "God is a partial God...for how many little children have died without baptism?" (Moroni 8:12) They are as pure as angels and saved from the foundation of the world, needing no baptism to reenter the kingdom of God, back into our Heavenly Father's loving arms.

These comforting words are full of hope to all who have lost a child in death. The Lord loves little children, for he tells us that "except ye be converted, and become as little children, ye shall not enter the kingdom of heaven." (Matthew 18:3)

My inner consciousness will be forever nourished with memories of these gentle moments among a gentle people.

16

Personal Testimony by Theophilus N. O. Pratt

(His own written words, June 1984)

How fascinating it is to realize that I share the most glorious opportunities with you as saints in the family of God in the worlds beyond the universe.

I cannot testify to any more truths in my life than to declare to you that I have made one of the greatest discoveries of the truths in life which is leading me and my family into that great happiness as hitherto unknown to me and others.

I shout and sing the Greek "Urika!" I have found it, that great happiness other sects of people are groping so laboriously for, through what they call mystics, burning candles and incense, applying all kinds of odours and colours, visiting graves and deserted places, spending money, learning incantations and chanting liturgy; and yet cannot find. Yes they cannot find it because they have no guidance, no prompting from the Holy Spirit, which with God, my Heavenly Father and his Only Begotten Son, Jesus Christ make the trinity—the Godhead, the Giver of all good things; gives to all men liberally and upbraideth not if they sincerely ask of him.

The Spirit of God like a fire is burning day and night within me, radiating into the life of my family and guiding us to live the gospel. At times I do falter, but no sooner than before, I see my shortcomings and retrace my newfound track to my Lord and friend, Jesus Christ, my King and my Saviour.

I pray to God, my Heavenly Father, that His guidance of the Holy Ghost which came upon me through the hands of Elder Folsom, on my priesthood ordination day should continue to burn in me and give me the power and sustain me to magnify my priesthood calling and exercise that same power of the Holy Ghost, the keys attached to it which I most conveniently hold.

Poor me, Pratt, a disgraceful, shameful sinner can now rebuke Satan, my former master who held me firmly by his chains—smoking, drinking, adultery, fornication, cheating and many more of those unrighteous conducts. I say I can now SHOUT Satan out and he runs from before me like a toothless bull. I pray simply and communicate with my Heavenly Father through Jesus Christ my Saviour, and my prayers are answered.

I would not commend myself; but I am proud that I am now a MORMON, a disciple of Prophet Joseph Smith (Jnr) and a sustainer of the only living prophet of God our Heavenly Father, President Spencer W. Kimball.

How come these wonderful realizations and achievements? Yes ACHIEVEMENTS, because only the faithful would have it and they would have it because they obey the commandments of God and live by the gospel principles.

I was born and bred Methodist until the middle part of July 1983. I never realized the need for moderation, the need for the Word of Wisdom, the principles of repentance to be followed by baptism through the hands of the proper authority for the remission of sins. But I knew how God had covenanted with the people in the Bible, but how did that matter to me? I could tell the Methodist congregation any of the stories in the Bible, the Gospels, and the parables of Jesus Christ, and many of his teachings. I was at that time "The DO what I say and NOT what I do" sort of preacher.

I give much thanks to Elder Williams who correctly introduced me to the Latter-day Saint approach to the scriptures. I remember this missionary pointing to the Bible I was holding and saying "You have the most beautiful books." I didn't know how a Bible I have been handling could look most beautiful to a white man.

These words from Elder Williams echoed in my ears and heart louder than before as the missionary continued to discuss other topics. Sister Williams was around and she shared the thrills of the conversation.

Further discussion led the missionary to invite me to his residence in Cape Coast. It was at the residence where for the first time I read the long name of the Church of which now I am a member. What a long name—"The Church of Jesus Christ of Latter-day Saints."

In my mind I started to tease and make fun of the name of the church. Out of ridicule I said why not Pounds, Pence, and Shillings (£ d S), the British currency?

I pondered on how much money I was to spend in order to meet the requirements of this " £d S" church. I decided to return to Moree without the Williams seeing me, that would only mean I did not honour the invitation. And what did that matter to me?

The expressions from Elder Williams echoed and rang more meaningfully to me: "Pratt, you have the most beautiful book," "You are a spirit son of your Heavenly Father," "Your body is a temple of God," "Baptism must be given you through the hands of the proper authority," "The Lord has a purpose for you," and "You are more important to the Lord now than before."

These expressions as they echoed simultaneously through my ears dragged me to the living room of the missionary. I could not realize how I entered the main hall. But there I stood receiving some sweet welcoming smiles from the Williams and the Folsoms.

The Folsoms had come to Ghana to release the Williams that very day. Those hearty welcoming smiles made me return a broad smile on my lips to my hosts. Elder Williams called me by name and introduced me to the Folsoms who immediately started a conversation with me. Sister Folsom was a good conversationalist. She took me through an informal discussion. Elder Folsom looked as if he had known me before this meeting. I was surprised at their "familiarity." Elder asked me to say the opening prayer. I did that. Elder Folsom breathed deep after the Amen and asked if he could begin with the discussion.

Soon I discovered that I was steadily being led into my investigation classes. I was astonished as to how practical the things of the Spirit were made so real and acceptable, that only a student with a biased mind, a polluted ideology, would ask questions. A hardened Methodist as I was I had questions to ask. The answers to the questions I asked proved that I was a religious illiterate and that I was just silly and stupid religiously and gospel-wise.

Thanks to the Folsoms for containing me and treating me with love, patience, endurance and all godly temperaments.

Without completing the course I felt I knew the new life as restored by Christ on earth; I asked for baptism from Elder Folsom. "Brother Pratt, you need to finish seven lessons and attend an interview before you will be baptized. I will not hesitate to baptize you," Elder Folsom replied.

And true to this assertion, there was much more to be investigated—the gift and work of the Holy Ghost, temple ordinances, the law of tithing, the truths behind the Word of Wisdom and facts on the resurrection of the body. I must show my gratitude to my Heavenly Father and his son Jesus Christ for instituting the restored Church of Jesus Christ on this earth and making me a student under the care of the Folsoms. Oh Lord, I praise thee and thank thee for these gifts.

On the day of my baptism the missionaries approved of a baptismal ground at Moree. Being proud of my redemption through faith in Jesus Christ, I was the only person baptized that day, backed by the Cape Coast Branch Choir who sang hymns from Zion.

Elder Folsom ushered me into the strait and narrow gate in the Lord's own restored Church to earth where there is a prophet, apostles, priests, teachers and deacons for the perfecting of the saints, for the work of the ministry, for the edifying of the body of Christ.

The knowledge that I have been accepted into the world-wide fellowship of The Church of Jesus Christ of Latter-day Saints made that day unique. Even though I became tongue-tied I was thrilled at the thought that I am a saint. I called myself lucky and saved through the atonement and salvation of my heavenly brother Jesus Christ who will come to judge the quick and the dead on his second coming.

I boldly testify that ever since my baptism my whole life has been prayerful, and I wait for the promptings of the Holy Ghost in all my activities. My close associates testify to this my claim and wonder how this change came by. I enjoy this newfound HAPPINESS with my wife and children. We look to Jesus as our friend, Saviour and Mediator. We have covenanted to do nothing without his counsel.

My baptism, confirmation and advancements into the service of The Church of Jesus Christ of Latter-day Saints are all pointers that my Heavenly Father, His Only Begotten Son and the Holy Ghost have a purpose for me and I am responsible to Him, His Son and the Holy Ghost.

In like manner the Lord has need of you. He loves you dearly. He is the Good Shepherd over you and His sheep. He knows you by name and he never says to the repentant "TOO LATE." He is ready even NOW. It is better to come now to meet your Saviour and friend, and enjoy the full happiness He has in store for you. Jesus is standing knocking at the door. When will you open the gates of your heart to receive him?

I testify that this restored Church of Jesus Christ of Latter-day Saints is true and that the only living prophet of God on earth is Spencer W. Kimball. I testify that President Spencer W. Kimball is a living interpreter of God on earth; and that the purpose of God for creating the world and the many wonderful living and non-living things on it is transmitted through him as his prophet; and that all men all over the world must heed his counsel so as to fulfill the plan of salvation God our Heavenly Father has in store for me and you.

I testify that those things as I say them are true, and in the hallowed name of my Saviour and friend, I pray.

Amen.

Tno N Pratt

T.N.O. PRATT

MOREE

17

My Conversion Story
by Emmanuel Emil Gyamfi

"Young man, I see a candle light before you. The Lord is going to use you for his work."

This was a night never to be forgotten. Life had become meaningless to me. As I lay musing about the purpose of life, I felt depressed in spirit. For years I had searched through books to find a fulfilling religion that could answer some pressing questions about life. Although born a Christian, I grew up to question the doctrines of the various Christian sects and the attitudes of the clergy who were supposed to lead their flock in the path of righteousness. To most Christians, religion to them meant Sunday worship and nothing else. It had ceased to mean the daily living of the gospel of Jesus Christ.

In consequence of this, I had completely ceased attending church and had no desire to affiliate with any Christian sect. However, my interest had been drawn to the Eastern philosophy such as Buddhism and for a time felt satisfied with some of the answers provided.

On the night mentioned, feeling depressed I decided to join a nearby prayer group for spiritual upliftment. It was the result of my joining them in prayer that the above message was given. I felt relieved and went home to enjoy a sound sleep. But then, I kept reflecting on the message as to the meaning of the Lord using me for his work. In any case, I let it rest at that.

On my return to Ghana from Nigeria in 1983, I visited an uncle whom I had missed for so long. In his study room I noticed some books on a shelf. Strangely, my hand was directed to a book with a blue cover, titled "The Book of Mormon." I quickly sat down to glance through it. After exchanging pleasantries with my uncle, I became deeply engrossed reading the book. Soon after, the following dialogue ensued between me and my uncle.

"Uncle, have you read this book?"

"I've read some few pages."

"Is it really true that Jesus appeared to this people on the American continent soon after his ascension to heaven?"

"Well, that is what the book says."

"I find it fascinating. Why haven't you read it through?"

"I guess it was rather drawing me away from my basic beliefs so I let it rest at that."

I felt truly overwhelmed by this wonderful story of Jesus visiting the American continent. It hit me like a thunderbolt to revolutionize my thinking. After leafing through the book for quite awhile, I put it back on the shelf promising myself to continue reading it on my next visit. On return to my uncle's place, I picked up the Book of Mormon again to read. I asked permission for the book to read at home. It took me three nights to finish reading through it. Here for the first time was the gospel of Jesus Christ succinctly explained. I enjoyed reading it tremendously. I read it over once more and got the message well planted in my heart.

But then, I asked myself, where can this "Church of Jesus Christ of Latter-day Saints" be found? Is it established only in the U.S.A.? I reasoned within myself that any church possessing a book having such a profound message like the Book of Mormon has something to be proud of. In any case I let the issue rest at that, cause I never thought that such a church could even be found in Africa, let alone my home town Cape Coast, Ghana.

A week or two later, I noticed a signboard indicating "The Church of Jesus Christ of Latter-day Saints" on an old dilapidated building which to all intents and purposes could not answer for a church building. This was a very strange encounter because I could not bring myself to believe that the church which owns the Book of Mormon was right at home to me. Then and there I decided to find out all about the church.

On a rainy Sunday morning, following this irresistible desire to find out about the Church, I went and quietly entered the chapel. As soon as I was seated, I developed a strange feeling of uneasiness. I went out and decided to leave. But then I had an inspiration to get back and stay until the service was over. This was a moment of decision and a moment I shall never forget. On reflection, I felt like the young Joseph Smith battling with the forces of darkness. I was completely torn between which voice to pay heed.

I kept standing outside the chapel, unable to decide whether to depart or get back to the chapel. A voice kept telling me to go back and wait till the service was over and make inquiries about the Church. Eventually I re-entered the chapel. Seated again, I became oblivious of what was taking place because I knew no one in the chapel and besides, the building had a leaky roof and there was a puddle on the floor. Where I sat, raindrops kept hitting my head. Was I receiving my first initiation into the Church? It seems to be so to me now.

At this time, I had bowed my head, not wanting anyone to notice "this stranger," as I thought myself. Suddenly I looked up, to see an old school mate conducting affairs at the podium. He was the branch president. I said to myself, "What is this fellow doing here?" My surprise at seeing him was due to the fact that he was once noted for fast living and being a man about town. For the first time, I breathed a sigh of relief, as I now knew someone I could contact to make inquiries. As soon as the service was over, I hurriedly went to meet him to make such inquiries. He was greatly surprised to find me at the church and asked how I got there since he didn't notice anyone accompanying me.

As soon as I replied that I had read the Book of Mormon and wanted to know all about the Church, he asked me to meet him at home so that he could furnish me with some tracts. I did, and never regretted doing so. I reflected on the message contained in the tracts, especially "The Testimony of the Prophet Joseph Smith." I sincerely believed the unique experience he underwent.

What a joy it was when I was finally introduced to the missionaries, Elder and Sister Williams. They patiently taught and inspired me in my efforts to find the truth. For the first time in my life I knew what truth is and how to pray. At the end of my indoctrination period, I knew the truth and had no choice but to be baptized.

The 17th day of June 1983 was my rebirth and dedication to the Lord. I pledged from then on I would spread the gospel news to anyone who would care to listen. Two months later, at a district conference, I was ordainded an elder and set apart as a branch clerk, and as a district missionary. I was offered three offices at the same time. This baffled me and brought to mind the prophetic message given me that the Lord was going to use me for his work.

This is truly the Lord's Church and I was called to sacrifice my quota towards the building of Zion in Ghana. Ever since my baptism the Holy Spirit has continued to testify to me the truthfulness of the restored gospel. It is my greatest delight as a district missionary to see how people's lives are transformed as they aspire to live the gospel of Jesus Christ.

One of the greatest testimonies I bear about the Church is the conversion of my twin brother into the Church in Denmark as a result of my persistent encouragement and prayer that the Lord testify of the truthfulness of the restored gospel to him. What a joy to have him continually testify of the miraculous happenings that have occurred in his life ever since he was baptized into the Church. The Church is truly the Lord's and it offers the greatest message for the salvation of man. My the rock which was cut out of the mountain without hands keep rolling thoughout eternity. Amen.

October 1984 Your son,

Emmanuel.

Emmanuel

When we met Emmanuel he had been baptized just four weeks previously, but had already attained a deep spiritual maturity. A man in his mid-thirties, he had a hunger for spiritual knowledge. In many long and in-depth gospel conversations in our home his probing queries, almost interrogations, revealed his eagerness to absorb and conform his life to gospel standards and principles.

He was among the first district missionaries called in Ghana, and was among those whom we trained in our home. He became a tireless, dedicated, and effective missionary. Along with the other Ghanaians called as missionaries, he fulfilled for his people the scripture that promised, "...every man shall hear the fulness of the gospel in his own tongue and in his own language..." (D & C 90:11)

Emmanuel brought many into the fold of Jesus Christ, among them were two uncles he proudly baptized. One, over 70-years old and the patriarch of his clan, assured us that many of his family would follow him. That is the manner in which it continually occurred in Ghana, just like "follow the leader." The other uncle asked Emmanuel, "How come you have this wonderful gospel and I've never even heard of it?" He was so thrilled with finding the gospel that he couldn't be baptized soon enough.

Shortly after our return home Emmanuel went to England to further pursue his education. There he received his temple ordinances and continues with his missionary zeal. He wrote: "It is my intention to leave for Zimbabwe to work and serve a part-time mission as well." As his "Mum and Dad," we could not have a finer son. He will always be held in deepest love and esteem in our hearts.

A profound statement expressed by Emmanuel, as he stood framed in our kitchen doorway, will always be remembered: "When we say that God cannot inspire other scriptures to be written we are limiting the power of God."

18

Farewell

Breathes there the man, with soul so dead,
Who never to himself hath said,
This is my own, my native land!
Whose heart hath ne'er within him burn'd,
As home his footsteps he hath turn'd
From wandering on a foreign strand!
(Sir Walter Scott: Lay of the Last Minstrel)

It was the most rewarding year of our lives—infused with so much spiritual joy—while at the same time the hardest; even as Charles Dickens succinctly stated: "It was the best of times—it was the worst of times." (The Tale of Two Cities)

Our feelings were mixed as we contemplated parting from beloved brothers and sisters we may never again meet in this life. But, if not here, then if we keep the faith, in a far better world for us all. Also, we left reluctantly, not having completed the chapel, but we knew that competent hands would continue the work.

The Sunday before our departure, President Cooper, in his final visit to Cape Coast (he too was leaving), presided at another noteworthy district conference. Our district was divided to make two: the Cape Coast and Takoradi Districts. Where there had been one district in all of Ghana with eight branches when we arrived, there were now four thriving districts with fourteen branches. The Accra District had also become two: the Accra and Kumasi Districts.

We were unprepared for the wonderful sendoff by the Cape Coast branches. An evening of entertainment included cultural dances, singing, drumming and dramas, with each branch presenting a charming play:

Old Cape Coast District Presidency. Left to right: Stephen A. Kwaw, President Kwelu P. Ghartey, Charles Kofi Ansah

New Cape Coast District Presidency. Left to right: William E. D. Acquah, first counselor; President Stephen Atimo Kwaw; Jim Nyankah, second counselor; Andrew Christian Coleman, clerk

> The children of Cape Coast Second Branch sensitively portrayed the apostasy with the apostles of Christ going forth to preach, being persecuted, and finally martyred.
>
> First Branch hilariously enacted the scenes of how an indigenous marriage was arranged, with relatives negotiating for a bride, the dowry, et al. Such hams! It was marvelous.
>
> The Coopers being present made it special. How do you measure the boundless blessings and experiences that have been ours throughout the past year? Laden with gifts we return, but the gifts of the spirit and heart far surpass anything material. (*Journal.*)

Another delightful and spontaneous farewell was provided by our neighbor's children, the Bafloes, on the day we departed. All eight of them, between the ages of four and eleven, seven little girls in their pretty dresses and one boy in shirt and shorts, sang songs and recited poetry in both English and Fante for about an hour. They were charming and were another reason why going away was difficult.

At the time of our leaving, a spirit of optimism seemed to be pervading the land, with hope for a brighter future, as noted on May 14th:

> Last year upon arrival, crops without rain were searing in the relentless heat. With quiet desperation people were more hungry looking; many more beggars on the street and at our doors. Now, after several good rains, crops are being planted everywhere. There's a feeling of hope that was absent last year. (*Journal.*)

And again, on June 5th, shortly before leaving:

> Heavy rains today, in fact several lately. My, this is making the crops grow. Have never seen the land so lush and promising. The Lord is truly blessing the land. The look of hunger and starvation does not stalk the land as it did. We rejoice for this. This is seen by the saints as a direct result of the Lord's blessings upon the land.

Being occupied with tasks inherent to departure kept my emotions in check as I anticipated the joyous reunion with our families; to give long awaited-grandma lovin' to grandchildren, especially to two newly arrived grandsons, Jordan Folsom and Brandon Becker.

The flight from Accra on British Caledonian, although exciting as we counted down the hours, was uneventful. At Schipol Airport in Amsterdam, Holland, a seven hour layover and a change to KLM Airline afforded a transition period to review and reacquaint ourselves with western culture.

The reunion was all and more than we had dreamed. A twenty-foot banner in the Salt Lake City airport proclaiming "WELCOME HOME" was a crowd stopper. Most of our children and grandchildren were there, just as when we had left.

We were thrilled, too, to again set foot on the land of the free and the home of the brave, the land of promise, the land of opportunity, the land to which almost everyone on earth yearns to come. This land is seen as truly a beacon light, a ray of hope from afar, by many beleaguered peoples suffering under oppression and privation.

Our much less important fantasies could now also be realized. Donna Nelson and I had at times speculated as to what we would eat when first we set foot in America and could have anything we desired. Would it be a glass of cold milk, ice cream, a tossed salad, a steak, or just a wonderfully pure drink of cool water right from the faucet or from the end of a garden hose? I'm sure the first taste of America was the fresh pure water. All else was not far behind.

The abundant and simple blessings of life we enjoy are so often taken for granted. Never, hopefully, will I be guilty of this again. We truly live in a land "choice above all others."

19

Epilogue

Write this for a memorial in a book
(Exodus 17:14)

Our experiences have elicited intense interest from all we've met. Each time we've shared them in firesides, schools, clubs, or sacrament meetings has renewed our love for the magnificent plan prepared and exemplified by our elder brother Jesus Christ, and for the loving arms of the Church spread out to bless his children into "the uttermost parts of the earth."

When asked to present a seminar on "How to Prepare for a Mission," I replied that it should be called, "How to Prepare for Life's Greatest Joys and Blessings." To those contemplating or yet reluctant to grasp this opportunity, let me share some of my happy discoveries:

- Be prepared to be healthy enough to spend the busiest year or more of your life, and to feel the Lord sustain your health and strength.
- Be prepared to financially sustain yourself, while at the same time (in many cases) spend less than you would at home.
- Be prepared to see your children and grandchildren grow spiritually, grow in love for you, for each other, and for the Lord, and to sustain each other in times of need.
- Be prepared to spend every waking moment for the Lord, lose yourself in the work and love it.
- Be prepared to see your priorities change and your love of material things fade as you distinguish your wants from your needs. You realize how silly it is to fret and struggle for "things."
- Be prepared to be led by the Spirit.

- Be prepared to be protected by the Lord.
- Be prepared to witness and experience spiritual manifestations, even miracles.
- Be prepared for your love of all peoples to expand mightily, remembering that love has no color or poverty line.
- Be prepared to use all your talents and training, regardless of how insignificant you regard them, in helping others. Older couples have experience that younger ones as yet do not. You will be capable of doing things you never thought possible. The Lord will help you succeed.
- Be prepared to change the lives of people and in return find love never before realized.
- Be prepared to have your own life changed forever. You will never be the same for you will see through different eyes and feel with a different heart.
- Be prepared to entertain angels in the form of General Authorities who may visit with you, or stay in your home. Never worry about what you don't have. They are humble servants of the Lord.
- Be prepared to leave your comfortable home and possessions behind, to give them barely a thought and while in humble surroundings, devoid of most comforts, find joy.
- Be prepared to see your love and appreciation grow for this blessed land of America, which in spite of flaws, is still the land of promise.
- Be prepared to go to the greatest mission on earth, because you know that is where the Lord needs your special talents.
- Be prepared to find it more difficult to leave your new brothers and sisters than it was to leave the ones you left at home.
- Be prepared to speak with your bishop and tell him you want these joys and blessings.

The list could go on. Don't rationalize why you can't serve the Lord. The Lord needs you!

Since we've been home we have learned that before the meeting house in Ghana was completed it became necessary to enlarge it due to increased membership. It was finally completed after two years of construction and now has a chapel, six classrooms, a fully equipped kitchen, library, Relief Society and Primary rooms, and is being shared by three of the six branches now in Cape Coast.

This lovely edifice was dedicated on 18 August, 1985 by Elder Neal A. Maxwell of the Council of the Twelve Apostles. This was indeed a momentous day for us, for the land of Ghana and especially for the saints who had prayed and worked diligently toward that eagerly sought goal. It was historic, as it marked the completion of the first building constructed in Ghana by the Church specifically as an LDS meeting house.

Cape Coast chapel as first completed (Photo by Carl Halladay).

Several days after the dedication we were overjoyed to hear Elder Maxwell on the telephone giving us a first hand report of the event. "What a marvelous experience," he said "to be among such soft, gentle people." He further stated that 1,300 people attended, with the overflow crowd accommodated in the open courtyard. Among those present were two full rows of village chieftains in full-dress regalia (what a splendid sight that must have been). Also in attendance were many civic and business leaders. He realized, he said, why we could truly love them, as he too found them to be a fine, wonderful people.

Soon the mails from Ghana brought messages relevant to this special occasion. Excerpts from a few depict their feelings:

> "Our beautiful edifice has become the talk of the town. It has brought many investigators into the Church." (J.W.B. Johnson)

"The occasion was unique and has gone into the archives of the Church. The chapel was full, with some under canopies outside the chapel. The apostle and his entourage were met on arrival by Primary children who gave him flowers and sang, 'I Am a Child of God.' We saw Elder Maxwell to be quiet, simple and meek. He spoke calmly and with conviction. His appearance really testifies that he is a special witness of our Lord Jesus Christ. I had the privilege of shaking his hand." (Kojo Amankwah)

"The beautiful edifice you helped us erect shall always stand as a strong testimony for your wonderful work in this Lord's vineyard. The chapel is so beautiful and well sited that it has become a cynosure of the whole locality." (Emmanuel E. Gyamfi)

"It was a grand occasion. We had an apostle of the Lord with us. I felt really blessed that day. The apostle's utterances were full of inspiration, and truly I have never had such a sweet experience in my life, as that day. A chief present asked about the Church and is now receiving lessons." (Anthony Borketey-Coffie)

"What a joy to have that great man of God with us." (Thomas Appiah, Jnr.)

Other letters continue to arrive bearing expressions of gratitude and fervent testimonies that will sustain and guide them onward and upward.

Since that day of dedication, many buildings in Ghana have been acquired by the Church and converted into suitable meeting houses. The progress in Africa has barely begun. We see the true gold in Ghana to be the rich harvest of souls. As the dark continent is aroused from slumber, the Church will be in the forefront to help develop its mighty potential, and there also it will be an ensign to the world.

Many Ghanaians, both young men and women, are now serving as full-time missionaries in their homeland, supplementing the work of the district missionaries. Also due to more favorable government regulations, the couple-missionary force from America has been permitted to substantially increase. The Ghanaian saints look forward steadfastly to stakehood and to that day when the prophetic words of Elder Derek A. Cuthbert will be fulfilled when he said a temple would be erected, wherein, if faithful, they could partake of the Lord's greatest blessings.

Also as announced in the 9 January, 1988, "Church News," a translation of selected parts of the Book of Mormon has been published in the Fante dialect of Akan. Priscilla Sampson-Davis who was doing the work when we were there, began the translation on her own and was assisted in the review by District President J.W.B. Johnson. This great blessing will nourish and inspire them as they continue to feast on the words of Christ.

"Now...we see that God is mindful of every people, whatsoever land they may be in; yea, he numbereth his people, and his bowels of mercy are over all the earth. Now this is my joy, and my great thanksgiving; yea, and I will give thanks unto my God forever. Amen." (Alma 26:37)

Bibliography

1. Aggrey, Dr. A.G. "Aggrey of Africa", Ghanaian philosopher, quoted in "Ghana: Past and Present" by Americo Samassa Mayer, [The Hague, Levisson Press]

2. Hymns 1985, The Church of Jesus Christ of Latter-day Saints [Salt Lake City, Utah]

3. The Church News (The Book of Mormon Fante Translation) 9 January 1988, p.3 Deseret News Publishing Co. 1988 [Salt Lake City, Utah]

4. The Encyclopedia Americana, International Edition 1963, International Headquarters, 575 Lexington Ave., [New York, New York]. Vol.2, p.10a.

5. The Ensign of The Church of Jesus Christ of Latter-day Saints, [Salt Lake City, Utah] October 1980 p.28.

6. World Vision Magazine, August-September 1984, p.23. Ted Engstrom, Publisher, World Vision Inc., [Monrovia, California]